W9-BYH-913

14

MASTER •THE Basics

RUSSIAN

Natalia Lusin, Ph.D.

BARRON'S

To Professor Nicholas Ozerov

All inquiries should be addressed to:
Barron's Educational Series, Inc.
250 Wireless Boulevard
Hauppauge, New York 11788

Library of Congress Catalog Card No. 95-78081
International Standard Book No. 0-8120-9164-7

Printed in the United States of America

5678 8800 987654321

Contents

PREFACE

This book is intended for students, businesspeople, and others interested in improving their knowledge of Russian. It can be used both to review material learned previously, and to learn new material. Definitions, explanations, and examples are given throughout. My intention is to provide a concise, yet comprehensive, grammar review that will be accessible to elementary, intermediate, and advanced students of Russian.

There are two tests in this book—one at the beginning, and one at the end. The first one helps students of Russian to determine the weak points in their knowledge of the language. They should then review the material in the main part of the book, the Grammar Brush-Up. Afterwards, by taking the review test that follows, they can determine how well the material was learned.

The main part of the book, the Grammar Brush-Up, is divided into three sections. "The Basics" covers some preliminary topics such as the alphabet, spelling, pronunciation, and rules of word order. "The Parts of Speech" presents Russian nouns, verbs, adjectives, and other classes of words. "Special Topics," the third section, covers terminology needed to talk about time, dates, weather, and health.

I would like to thank Dimitry Popow and Grace Freedson of Barron's for all their help with this project. If readers have any suggestions or comments on this book, they should write to me in care of the publisher.

Natalia Lusin

HOW TO USE THIS BOOK

In the chapters that follow, a numerical decimal system has been used with the symbol § in front of it. This was done so that you may find the reference to a particular point in basic Russian grammar more easily by using the index. For example, if you look up the entry "nouns" in the index, you will find the reference given as §9. Sometimes additional § reference numbers are given when the entry you consult is mentioned in other areas.

FIND OUT WHAT YOU KNOW

Take the test on the following pages before studying any of the material in this book. The results of the test will help you to determine your current strengths and weaknesses in Russian grammar.

The test consists of 60 questions that are divided into 3 sections. Each section corresponds to a section in the Grammar Brush-Up (the central part of this book).

After you take the test, correct it by using the answer key that follows the test. Then fill out the Diagnostic Analysis chart to determine the topics in the Grammar Brush-Up that will require the greatest attention from you. If you want to review material that relates to one specific answer, check the number listed after each answer.

At the end of the book, there is another test. It is divided by chapter and consists of 379 questions. You can take the test in its entirety after you have reviewed all of the Grammar Brush-Up, or you can review the material and test yourself chapter by chapter.

Although the two tests are meant to be useful guides for study, they of course cannot cover all of the material in the Grammar Brush-Up. Even if you answer all of the questions for a particular topic correctly, do not ignore that topic. Review it after you have reviewed the topics with which you had problems.

Test Yourself

Answer as many of the questions below as you can. Do not look at the answer key until you have finished.

THE BASICS

1. The letter ц is pronounced like the highlighted letters in
   A. **sh**ape □
   B. **ch**ase □
   C. ba**ts** □

2. The letter **у** is pronounced like the highlighted letter(s) in
   A. to**y**   ☐
   B. s**oo**n   ☐
   C. **you**   ☐
3. The letter **ы** can be written after the letter **ш**. True or false? _____
4. The letter **и** can be written after the letter **г**. True or false? _____
5. When the letter **о** is in an unstressed syllable immediately before the stressed syllable of a word, it is pronounced like
   A. **а**   ☐
   B. **о**   ☐
   C. **и**   ☐
6. If a voiced consonant has a voiceless counterpart, it will be pronounced like that voiceless consonant when it appears at the end of a word. True or false? _____
7. In Russian, the names of days and months are not capitalized. True or false? _____
8. Because Russian does not have definite and indefinite articles, your decision to use "a" or "the" when translating into English will be based on
   A. context   ☐
   B. word order   ☐
   C. context and/or word order ☐
9. Translate into Russian.
   Tanla is a professor. _____
10. Where must the negative particle **не** be placed in a sentence?
    A. immediately before the word it negates   ☐
    B. immediately after the word it negates   ☐
    C. at the beginning of the sentence   ☐
11. If a person's first name is Pavel and his father's name is Alexander, what is the correct way to address him formally? _____
12. When you are introduced to the mother of a friend, would it be correct to use **вы** or **ты** to address her?
    A. **вы**   ☐
    B. **ты**   ☐

PARTS OF SPEECH

Fill in the blanks by putting the words in parentheses into the appropriate case for each sentence.

13. Ка́тя чита́ет _____. (кни́га)
14. На столе́ лежи́т _____. (каранда́ш)

15. Са́ша и Пе́тя говоря́т о _____. (спорт)
16. В э́той кварти́ре мно́го _____. (окно́)
17. Мы прие́дем в Нью-Йо́рк _____. (авто́бус)
18. Четы́ре _____ гуля́ли в па́рке. (де́вочка)
19. Вчера́ Ми́ша написа́л письмо́ _____. (друзья́)

20. The following is an example of an interrogative adjective.
    A. ста́рый ☐
    B. чьи ☐
    C. на́ше ☐
    D. э́та ☐

21. The following is an example of a comparative adjective.
    A. бо́лен ☐
    B. ма́ленькая ☐
    C. са́мый хоро́ший, ☐
    D. бо́лее интере́сные ☐

Translate the following into Russian.

---

22. my big house _____
23. this lamp _____
24. the future _____

25. The following is an example of a personal pronoun.
    A. себя́ ☐
    B. что-то ☐
    C. они́ ☐
    D. сам ☐

26. The following is an example of a negative pronoun.
    A. кото́рая ☐
    B. никто́ ☐
    C. чего́ ☐
    D. них ☐

27. The following is an example of an interrogative pronoun.
    A. кому́ ☐
    B. мне ☐
    C. са́ми ☐
    D. себе́ ☐

28. The verbs in the sentence, Ле́на прочита́ла газе́ту и написа́ла письмо́, are
    A. imperfective ☐
    B. perfective ☐

29. Fill in the following charts.

работать (present tense)	
я	мы
ты	вы
он, оно́, она́	они́

люби́ть (present tense)	
я	мы
ты	вы
он, оно́, она́	они́

Translate the following into Russian.

---

30. I want to read. _____

31. Open the door! _____

32. The verb in the sentence, Де́ти хо́дят в шко́лу ка́ждый день, is
    A. determinate   ☐
    B. indeterminate   ☐

33. Translate into Russian.
    Who put the book on the floor? _____

    _____

34. The following is an example of a present active participle.
    A. говори́вшие   ☐
    B. бро́шенная   ☐
    C. ви́димое   ☐
    D. чита́ющий   ☐

Fill in the blanks with the appropriate Russian adverbs.

---

35. Мы уе́дем _____. (in the morning)

36. Она́ говори́т _____. (quietly)

37. На́до идти́ _____. (forward)

> Translate the following, writing out the numbers in Russian.

38. 321 cars _____
39. 74 big tables _____
40. 5,896 American students _____
41. The eighth day _____
42. We have two children _____

> Fill in the blanks by translating the words in parentheses.

43. Вася был _____. (at the store)

44. Я кончила работу _____. (in a day)

45. In Russian, the conjunction "but" is
    A. ли   ☐
    B. если   ☐
    C. но   ☐
    D. пока   ☐

46. In Russian, the conjunction "or" is
    A. или   ☐
    B. или . . . или   ☐
    C. ни . . . ни   ☐
    D. когда   ☐

47. In Russian, the interjection for "yuck" or "ick" is
    A. ой   ☐
    B. тс   ☐
    C. ага   ☐
    D. фу   ☐

> SPECIAL TOPICS

48. The addition of the prefix **не-** to the adjective **большой**
    A. changes its meaning   ☐
    B. changes its case   ☐
    C. changes it from an adjective to a noun   ☐

49. **-ист** is a suffix for
    A. adjectives   ☐
    B. nouns   ☐

50. The idiomatic expression, Клин клином вышибать, means
    A. to go too far   ☐
    B. to give as good as one gets   ☐
    C. to fight fire with fire   ☐

> Write out the following times in Russian.

51. Который час? Сейчас
_____ . (11:00)

52. Который час? Сейчас
_____ . (3:10)

53. Который час? Сейчас
_____ . (6:45)

54. Который час? Сейчас
_____ . (2 p.m.)

> Translate the following, writing out the numbers in Russian.

55. Today is Wednesday. _____

56. Today is May sixth. _____

57. 1924 _____

58. He is flying in on Friday, April 17th. _____
_____

59. The sentence, Идёт снег, means
    A. it's raining   ☐
    B. it's snowing   ☐
    C. it's going to snow   ☐

60. The sentence, У меня грипп, means
    A. I have a toothache   ☐
    B. my back hurts   ☐
    C. I have the flu   ☐

ANSWERS

RIGHT	WRONG		
_____	_____	1. C	see §1
_____	_____	2. B	see §1
_____	_____	3. False	see §2
_____	_____	4. True	see §2
_____	_____	5. A	see §3
_____	_____	6. True	see §3
_____	_____	7. True	see §4
_____	_____	8. C	see §5
_____	_____	9. Таня профёссор or	
		Таня—профёссор	see §6
_____	_____	10. A	see §7
_____	_____	11. Павел	
		Александрович	see §8
_____	_____	12. A	see §8

_____	_____	13. кни́гу	see §9.3-2
_____	_____	14. каранда́ш	see §9.3-1
_____	_____	15. спо́рте	see §9.3-4
_____	_____	16. о́кон	see §9.3-3
_____	_____	17. авто́бусом	see §9.3-6
_____	_____	18. де́вочки	see §9.3-3
_____	_____	19. друзья́м	see §9.3-5
_____	_____	20. B	see §10.5-4
_____	_____	21. D	see §10.5-5
_____	_____	22. мой большо́й дом	see §10.5-1 and 10.5-2
_____	_____	23. э́та ла́мпа	see §10.5-3
_____	_____	24. бу́дущее	see §10.5-7
_____	_____	25. C	see §11.2
_____	_____	26. B	see §11.8
_____	_____	27. A	see §11.3
_____	_____	28. B	see §12.4
_____	_____	29.	see §12.5-2

рабо́тать (present tense)	
я рабо́таю	мы рабо́таем
ты рабо́таешь	вы рабо́таете
он, оно́, она́ рабо́тает	они́ рабо́тают

люби́ть (present tense)	
я люблю́	мы лю́бим
ты лю́бишь	вы лю́бите
он, оно́, она́ лю́бит	они́ лю́бят

_____	_____	30. Я хочу́ чита́ть.	see §12.6 and 12.7
_____	_____	31. Откро́й дверь! **or** Откро́йте дверь!	see §12.8
_____	_____	32. B	see §12.11
_____	_____	33. Кто положи́л кни́гу на пол?	see §12.12
_____	_____	34. D	see §12.13
_____	_____	35. у́тром	see §13.4

____ ____	36. тихо	see §13.4
____ ____	37. вперёд	see §13.4
____ ____	38. триста двадцать	
	одна машина	see §14.1
____ ____	39. семьдесят четыре	
	больших стола	see §14.1
____ ____	40. пять тысяч восемьсот	
	девяносто шесть	
	американских	
	студентов	see §14.1
____ ____	41. восьмой день	see §14.2
____ ____	42. У нас двое детей	see §14.3
____ ____	43. в магазине	see §15.3
____ ____	44. за день	see §15.3
____ ____	45. C	see §16
____ ____	46. A	see §16
____ ____	47. D	see §17
____ ____	48. A	see §18
____ ____	49. B	see §18
____ ____	50. C	see §19
____ ____	51. одиннадцать	
	часов	see §20
____ ____	52. десять минут	
	четвёртого	see §20
____ ____	53. без четверти семь	see §20
____ ____	54. два часа дня	see §20
____ ____	55. сегодня среда	see §21
____ ____	56. сегодня шестое	
	мая	see §21
____	57. тысяча девятьсот	
	двадцать четвёртый	
	год	see §21
____ ____	58. Он прилетит в	
	пятницу семнад-	
	цатого апреля	see §21
____ ____	59. B	see §22
____ ____	60. C	see §22

DIAGNOSTIC ANALYSIS

Section	Question Numbers	Number of Answers	
		Right	**Wrong**
THE BASICS			
1. The Russian Alphabet	1, 2		
2. The Spelling Rules	3, 4		
3. Pronunciation	5, 6		
4. Mechanics	7		
5. The Absence of Articles	8		
6. The Absence of the Verb "to be" in the Present Tense	9		
7. Word Order	10		
8. Names and the Use of ты and вы	11, 12		
THE PARTS OF SPEECH			
9. Nouns	13, 14, 15, 16, 17, 18, 19		
10. Adjectives	20, 21, 22, 23, 24		
11. Pronouns	25, 26, 27		
12. Verbs	28, 29, 30, 31, 32, 33, 34		
13. Adverbs	35, 36, 37		
14. Numbers	38, 39, 40, 41, 42		
15. Prepositions	43, 44		
16. Conjunctions	45, 46		
17. Interjections	47		
SPECIAL TOPICS			
18. Word Formation	48, 49		
19. Idioms	50		
20. Telling Time	51, 52, 53, 54		
21. Dates, Days, Months, Seasons	55, 56, 57, 58		
22. Talking about the Weather, Health	59, 60		
TOTAL QUESTIONS:	60		

Use the following scale to see how you did.

55 to 60 right:	Excellent
50 to 54 right:	Very Good
45 to 49 right:	Average
40 to 44 right:	Below Average
Fewer than 40 right:	Unsatisfactory

A GRAMMAR BRUSH-UP
The Basics
§1.

The Russian Alphabet

The Russian alphabet, which contains 33 letters, is not as difficult to learn as it may appear. Some letters (for example, a and o) are the same as English ones, or are very similar (for example, к). Some (for example, в) look like English letters but represent other sounds in Russian. Others (for example, ж) bear no resemblance to English letters and must be learned from scratch.

The English words given below contain sounds that provide an approximate pronunciation of the Russian letters.

Printed Letter	Written Letter	Pronounced as in the English:
А а	*Аа*	car
Б б	*Бб*	**b**ook
В в	*Вв*	**v**erse
Г г	*Гг*	**g**o
Д д	*Дg*	**d**og
Е е	*Ее*	**ye**ll
Ё ё	*Ёё*	**yo**ur
Ж ж	*Жж*	mea**s**ure
З з	*Зз*	**z**oo
И и	*Ии*	**s**treet
Й й	*Йй*	**toy**

Printed Letter	Written Letter	Pronounced as in the English:
К к	*Кк*	bake
Л л	*Лл*	long
М м	*Мм*	**m**any
Н н	*Нн*	**n**o
О о	*Оо*	f**o**r
П п	*Пп*	**s**port
Р р	*Рр*	see §3
С с	*Сс*	**s**un
Т т	*Тт*	**t**ime
У у	*Уу*	s**oo**n
Ф ф	*Фф*	**f**un
Х х	*Хх*	**h**at
Ц ц	*Цц*	ba**ts**
Ч ч	*Чч*	**ch**ase
Ш ш	*Шш*	**sh**ape
Щ щ	*Щщ*	di**sh ch**ips
ъ	*ъ*	hard sign—see §3
ы	*ы*	p**i**g
ь	*ь*	soft sign—see §3
Э э	*Ээ*	g**e**t
Ю ю	*Юю*	**you**
Я я	*Яя*	**ya**rn

Letters for which no capitals are given never occur at the beginning of a word—capitals are therefore unnecessary.

You need to write in script when you write Russian—Russians do not use the printed alphabet when writing by hand.

Note which letters rise above the midline and which do not. Note also which letters fall below the lower line. In script, the loops on *и* and *ш* go off to the side and are considerably smaller than the script loops on *g*, *з*, and *у*. Keep the initial script hooks on *л*, *м*, and *я* small, but be sure that they are there. Otherwise, letters will run into each other and will be hard to read: *шум*.

In actual practice, people do not write with great precision. For ease of reading, it helps to draw a line under *ш* and over *m* (in their lower-case script forms) in order to distinguish between them: *тише*.

When writing *ш* be sure to bring the last stroke down completely: it should not resemble the English letter w. The lower-case script versions of *ə* and *ч* are similar, but remember that *ч* is flat on top, while *ə* is curved.

All letters are joined in script (except *л*, *м*, and *я* when preceded by *о*). In some cases, a short diagonal dash may connect two letters: *дань*.

§2. The Spelling Rules

Certain vowels cannot be written after certain consonants.

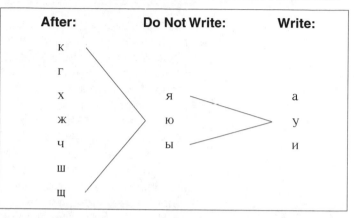

After:	Do Not Write:	Write:
к		
г		
х	я	а
ж	ю	у
ч	ы	и
ш		
щ		

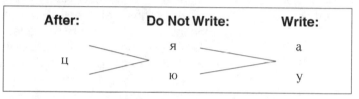

After:	Do Not Write:	Write:
ц	я	а
	ю	у

Use ы after ц in endings. In the roots of most words, и can be used after ц.

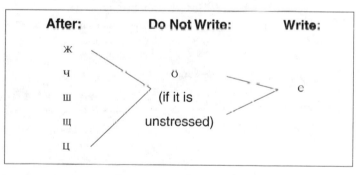

After:	Do Not Write:	Write:
ж		
ч	о	
ш	(if it is	е
щ	unstressed)	
ц		

§3. Pronunciation

The pronunciation of a letter is affected by its position in a word, the surrounding letters, and the location of the stress. (In English, there can be a secondary stress in a word—in Russian, there is only one stress per word.) If a vowel is stressed, it is pronounced as indicated in the chart in §1. If it is unstressed, it may be pronounced somewhat differently.

When unstressed and located in the syllable immediately before the stressed syllable, о and а are pronounced like a less distinct а (see chart in §1). The same holds true when а or о is the initial letter of a word. When unstressed and located in any other position, о and а are pronounced "uh."

When unstressed and following a soft consonant, both я and е are pronounced like и (see chart in §1).

И is pronounced like ы after ж, ш, and ц and when it is the initial letter of a word preceded by a word that ends in a hard consonant: Вадим играет. (Vadim is playing.) In all other positions, stressed or unstressed, it is pronounced as indicated in §1.

The vowels э, ю, у, and ы are also pronounced as indicated in §1, whether they are stressed or unstressed.

The letter ё is always stressed, so it is unaffected by these distinctions.

Vowels are paired and are conventionally termed "hard" and "soft":

Hard:	а	у	ы	о	э
Soft:	я	ю	и	ё	е

With the exception of и, when a soft vowel is the first letter of a word, or when it follows another vowel or the letters ь and ъ, it has a distinct sound like the English "y" at the beginning (е—as in **ye**ll, я—as in **ya**rn) and therefore consists of two sounds. When a soft vowel comes after a consonant, it palatalizes, or softens, that consonant (this does not apply to consonants that cannot be softened—see below).

Palatalization involves placing the middle of the tongue against the middle of the roof of the mouth when pronouncing the letter. English speakers generally find it hard to pronounce palatalized consonants at first, and they may also find it hard to distinguish between palatalized and nonpalatalized consonants when listening to Russian. The ability to tell the difference develops gradually.

Hard vowels do not have a "y" sound at the beginning and do not palatalize consonants.

The Soft Sign

Consonants are softened not only by soft vowels, but also when followed by the soft sign. The soft sign has no sound in and of itself, but it palatalizes the consonant that precedes it. (It can never be written after a vowel.)

Most consonants can be softened by using a soft sign or a soft vowel. However, ж, ш, and ц are always hard. If a soft sign or soft vowel is written after them, then it is simply a spelling convention. It does not affect their pronunciation. The consonants ч, щ, and й are always soft. Their pronunciation is also unaffected by spelling.

к, г, and х are softened by soft vowels, never by the soft sign.

The Hard Sign

The hard sign occurs much less frequently than the soft sign. Like the soft sign, it has no sound in and of itself, and it can be written only after consonants. Its purpose is not to harden consonants: it separates a consonant from the soft vowel that follows and thereby allows the soft vowel to preserve its initial "y" sound, which would ordinarily be lost after a consonant. (The soft sign, when located between a consonant and a soft vowel, also performs this kind of separation function.)

Consonants are divided into voiced and voiceless. Voiced consonants are produced through vibration of the vocal cords; voiceless consonants are produced without that vibration. Some voiced consonants have voiceless counterparts:

Voiced:	б	в	г	д	ж	з
Voiceless:	п	ф	к	т	ш	с

Each pair of consonants above represents the same articulation, but one is produced by using the vocal cords, while the other is not.

Some consonants do not have counterparts:

Voiced	**Voiceless**
л м н р й	х ч щ ц

If a voiced consonant has a voiceless counterpart, it will be pronounced like that voiceless consonant in certain situations.

1. It will be pronounced as voiceless when it appears at the end of a word: год [got]; but го́ды [gody] (year; years).

2. It may also be pronounced as voiceless in a consonant cluster. In Russian, when two consonants appear together, the second consonant affects the first. Therefore, if the second one is voiceless, then the first one is also pronounced as voiceless: ло́дка [lotka] (boat).

It is also true that if the second consonant is voiced, the first consonant is pronounced as voiced: сдать [zdat'] (to pass).

Because a preposition and the word that follows it are pronounced as one word, the same pronunciation rules on consonant clusters apply there: с Бори́сом [z Borisom]; из Ту́лы [is Tuly] (with Boris; from Tula).

In a consonant cluster of more than two consonants, one consonant may not be pronounced. In здра́вствуй [zdrastvuj] (hello), the first в is left out in pronunciation. In со́лнце [sontse] (sun), the л is not pronounced.

There is a consonant phoneme in Russian that is linguistically designated as "j" ("jot"). It is pronounced like the y in yes and is represented in Russian with different symbols.

When it is the last letter of a word, or when it appears before a consonant, it is written as й. When it occurs before a vowel, it is spelled with a soft vowel. For example:

moj → мой
moj + a → моя (my)

When j comes after a consonant *and* before a vowel, it requires both a soft sign and a soft vowel:

pjot → пьёт ([he/she] drinks)

(After prefixes, the hard sign is used instead of the soft sign to designate the presence of j.)

The Russian letter р is different in pronunciation from the English letter r. Although the tongue is in basically the same position for both letters, it vibrates for the pronunciation of р but does not for r.

When г occurs in the ending -ого, it is pronounced like в: кра́сного [krasnovo] (red).

As stated above, Russian words have only one stress per word. The speaker's tone rises until the stressed syllable is reached, then it falls. A similar thing happens in sentences: generally, the pitch of the speaker's voice falls after the stressed syllable of the most important word in the sentence is reached.

Modern Russian grammar books usually provide students with four "intonational contours," or intonational curves. Each contour is used for certain types of sentences.

Здесь живёт Ка́тя.
(Katya lives here.)

IC-1—used for declarative sentences

Куда́ вы идёте?
(Where are you going?)

IC-2—used for interrogative sentences that have an interrogative word

Э́то твоя́ кни́га?
(Is this your book?)

IC-3—used for interrogative sentences that do not have an interrogative word

А Са́ша?
(And Sasha?)

IC-4—used for incomplete interrogative sentences containing "а." These sentences are usually part of a series of questions

Stress

No well-defined rules govern the placement of stress in Russian. As a result, most introductory and intermediate texts, including this one, mark the stress of words that have more than one syllable. (Since ё is always stressed, words containing that letter need not be marked.)

A few general guidelines, however, may be helpful:

1. Most nouns do not change stress when they change case.

2. Long-form adjectives do not change stress when they change case. (For more on other adjectival forms and stress, see the appropriate section in §10.)

3. Pronouns are usually stressed on the ending.

4. Some present tense verbs are stressed on the same syllable of the stem or ending in all six forms. In other verbs, the stress falls on the same syllable of the stem in all forms except the first person singular ("I"), where the ending is stressed.

5. For the past tense forms, most verbs have the same stress as the infinitive, but if a verb is monosyllabic (has one syllable), it is generally stressed on the ending in the feminine form.

Some Fine Points of Stress

Some masculine nouns shift stress to the ending in cases other than the nominative singular. Because there is no ending in the nominative singular, there can be no end stress in that case. Masculine nouns that take the -a/-я ending in the nominative plural are stressed on the ending in all cases of the plural.

Some neuter nouns have the same stress in all cases of the singular, then shift it to another syllable for all cases in the plural.

A fairly small, but frequently used group of feminine nouns has stress shift in some cases of both the singular and the plural. The stress patterns for these words must be memorized. If a word has variable stress, a good dictionary will list the stress for all the cases.

Perfective verbs with the prefix вы- are always stressed on the prefix.

Sometimes a preposition or particle is pronounced together with the following word as one word, with one stress, which falls on the preposition or particle: нé были ([they] were not [there]).

Stress in Russian is a difficult subject. The guidelines above should be studied, and the stress for each word must be learned when the word itself is memorized. It is worth the effort: incorrect stress may lead you to say something that you did not intend. For example, мукá means flour, while мýка means torment.

§4.

Mechanics

§4.1 CAPITALI-ZATION

As in English, the names of people and places are capital-ized in Russian. Capitalization is less common in Russian than in English, however. In Russian, do not capitalize days of the week, months of the year, names of languages and religions, and nouns and adjectives of nationality: понедéльник, пóльский язы́к, францу́з (Monday, Polish language, Frenchman).

Forms of address (for example, профéссор [Professor]) are also not capitalized. Although "I" is capitalized in English, in Russian "я" is not. When writing titles of works, capitalize the first word (and names of people and places), but use lower-case for subsequent words: Войнá и мир *(War and Peace)*.

§4.2 SYLLABIFI-CATION

There are as many syllables in a word as there are vowels in it. A single consonant forms a syllable with the vowel that follows it:

ре- кá (river)

Generally, in a consonant cluster, the last consonant forms a syllable with the vowel that follows:

пóл- ка (shelf)

The consonant й is always part of the same syllable as the vowel that precedes it:

лéй- ка (watering can)

When carrying part of a word to another line, always break the word at a syllable break. There is one restriction: a syllable may consist of a vowel alone (ó- ко- ло [near]), but a single vowel cannot remain alone on a line or be car-ried over alone.

§4.3 PUNCTUATION

In Russian, the same punctuation marks are used as in English, and in much the same way. There are, however, a few extra rules to keep in mind.

1. Subordinate clauses must always be set off by a comma:

Я не знáю, что мне дéлать. (I don't know what to do.)

2. Dialogue in a text may be marked by quotation marks
or by a dash. In Russian, the opening quotation mark is
placed at the bottom of the line and turned out: „ . Angled
brackets sometimes take the place of quotation marks: « ».
When a dash is used, it occurs at the beginning of the
quote only:

—Кто это? ("Who is that?")

§5.

The Absence of Articles

Russian does not have definite and indefinite articles, that is, it has no words for "a" and "the." When you translate into English, however, you should add them. Whether you choose "the" or "a" will depend on context and word order. For example, in Russian, new information tends to appear at the end of the sentence (see §7 for more on word order). In the sentence Учитель говорит с учеником, ученик (student) may be new information, while учитель (teacher) may be old information. Context will help to confirm this:

> Я жду моего старого учителя. Мне нужно с ним поговорить. Но я вижу, что **учитель говорит с учеником.** (I am waiting for my old teacher. I need to talk to him. But I see that **the teacher is talking with a student.**)

Before the last sentence is reached, the teacher has been mentioned and described. His existence is old information for the reader, and учитель is therefore translated with the definite article, "the." But ученик comes up for the first time in the last sentence, and no information is provided up to this point. It is translated with the indefinite article "a."

In some situations, there will be insufficient information to decide whether "a" or "the" should be used. In such a case, either one will do.

§6.

The Absence of the Verb "to be" in the Present Tense

The verb быть (to be) is usually not written in the present tense in Russian. It is, however, understood to be present and should be translated:

Андрей — студент. (Andrei is a student.)
Это дом. (This is a house.)

Sometimes a dash is written in the place where the verb would be.

Most forms of быть simply do not exist in the present tense:

я ———	мы ———
ты ———	вы ———
он / она́ есть	они ———

Есть is used rather infrequently. It is needed in long sentences to avoid possible confusion: it is seen, for example, in scientific definitions. It is also needed when the existence of someone or something needs to be underscored (and есть will be used even if the subject is plural):

У нас есть книги. (We have some books.)

(For more on the "у + the genitive" construction, see the section on prepositions in §9.3-3.)

The verb являться (to appear, to be) can be used as well. In contrast to быть, it exists in all six forms of the present tense. It is, however, rather formal and would not be used in conversations of the more casual sort (except when used in the meaning "to appear").

§7.

Word Order

Word order in sentences is freer in Russian than in English. The subject of a sentence may appear in the beginning, middle, or end of the sentence. Such flexibility is possible because of the Russian case system—the case endings tell you which word is the subject, which the object, and so forth. There are, however, some limitations. Some word order patterns are fairly common and are considered standard. Any departure from these patterns would sound somewhat unusual, although the sentence would not be grammatically incorrect. For example, Máша читáет газéту (Masha is reading the paper) follows the word order subject-verb-object, which is most common for such sentences. The word order Газéту читáет Máша will be encountered less frequently, but it may be necessary in certain situations. In answers to questions, for example, new information should come last:

—Кто читáет газéту? —Газéту читáет Máша. ("Who is reading the paper?" "Masha is reading the paper.")

Some parts of speech have certain restrictions on their position:

1. Interrogative words come first in a sentence—

Где вы бы́ли? (Where were you?)

2. The negative particle не immediately precedes the word that it negates—

Он взял не карандáш, а рýчку. (He took the pen, not the pencil.)

3. Generally, adjectives that agree come before the nouns that they modify. (See §10 for more information on adjectives. There are many different kinds, and some can take several positions.)

4. Adverbs generally go before the words that they modify—

Онá хорошó прочитáла доклáд. (She read the lecture well.)

If the adverb is placed at the end of the sentence, it tends to carry more emphasis.

5. Pronouns tend not to be placed at the end of a sentence—

Ми́тя нас ви́дел. (Mitya saw us.)

§8.

Names and the Use of Ты **and** Вы

Names

Russians do not have middle names: they are given only one name at birth. They also have a patronymic, which is not to be confused with a middle name. It is the full name of their father with a special ending attached (for a full list of endings, see below).

The full first name and patronymic are used when an individual must be addressed formally. This is the equivalent of Mr. —— or Ms. —— in English. Keep in mind that because this is a formal mode of address, nicknames cannot be used in its formation.

A person's full or given name can be turned into different kinds of nicknames, using a seemingly infinite collection of suffixes. These nicknames can be quite confusing to the non-native, owing to their variety. Furthermore, they do not always look like the name from which they are derived (Алекса́ндр—Са́ша, Влади́мир—Во́ва). Nicknames have emotional content as well: some nickname endings imply affection for the person addressed, others are fairly neutral, still others can indicate good-natured teasing, and some reflect hostility or criticism. As with names in general, some nicknames are fairly common, while others are infrequently encountered.

Russian last names present problems for students because some of the case endings are adjectival. The only thing to do is to memorize the endings for last names well. The most common Russian last names end in -ов/-ев or -ин (for -(ск)ий last names, see below) and have the following declension (forms with adjectival endings are in bold-face):

Case	Masculine	Feminine	Plural
Nom.	Ивано́в	Ивано́ва	Ивано́вы
Acc.	Ивано́ва	Ивано́ву	**Ивано́вых**
Gen.	Ивано́ва	Ивано́вой	**Ивано́вых**

Case	Masculine	Feminine	Plural
Prep.	Ивано́ве	Ивано́вой	Ивано́вых
Dat.	Ивано́ву	Ивано́вой	Ивано́вым
Inst.	Ивано́вым	Ивано́вой	Ивано́выми

Last names that end in -(ск)ий are declined like adjectives in all cases, genders, and numbers (see §10 for a chart of adjectival endings). Those that do not end in -ов/ -ев, -ин or -(ск)ий but in a consonant are not declined at all in the feminine or plural, but they are declined like masculine animate nouns in the masculine gender.

There is a historical reason for the presence of adjectival endings in last names—they are not an unexplainable peculiarity. See Genevra Gerhart's book *The Russian's World* (Harcourt Brace Jovanovich, 1974) for a good explanation of Russian last names, patronymics, and first names, as well as an extensive list of nickname variations.

First names are declined like other nouns (see §9 for more details), as are patronymics. Patronymics are formed by adding the following endings to the father's name:

ович — used for male children when the father's name ends in a hard consonant

евич — used for male children when the father's name ends in a soft consonant

овна — used for female children when the father's name ends in a hard consonant

евна — used for female children when the father's name ends in a soft consonant

For example:

Игорь Алекса́ндрович, Анна Алекса́ндровна (father—Алекса́ндр, son—Игорь, daughter—А́нна).

If a name ends in -й, the -й is not written in the patronymic: Серге́й — Серге́евич/Серге́евна.

Some names have exceptional forms of the patronymic: Па́вел — Па́влович/Па́вловна, Пётр — Петро́вич/ Петро́вна, Илья́ — Ильи́ч/Ильи́нична, Лев — Льво́вич/ Льво́вна, Михаи́л — Миха́йлович/Миха́йловна.

Ты / Вы

Americans are sometimes confused by the distinction between the "informal you" (ты) and the "formal you" (вы) in

Russian, since no such distinction exists in English. Generally speaking, children, family members, and close friends are addressed as ты and by their first name or nickname. (However, two people may be close friends and still address each other as вы, owing to a large age difference, a preference for formality, or some other reason.) Adults who are not close friends or family members are addressed as вы. They can be called by their name and patronymic (used in many business situations, for example), name only (acceptable in most social gatherings, provided the people are of the same age), or, occasionally, nickname (quite casual, and acceptable, for example, for a long-standing social acquaintance).

Educational background plays a role in the ты/вы choice—people with less education tend to choose to use ты in more situations than people with more education. Time is a factor as well—ты is used more frequently now than 50 or 100 years ago, a reflection of the growing informality of society.

People sometimes use вы when they first get to know a person, then switch to ты as they become more closely acquainted. Such a shift usually occurs only if the people involved are of the same generation and if the relationship is not a formal business or professional relationship. The shift to ты must come early in an acquaintance, or else it is unlikely to take place, since the people involved will have become too accustomed to using вы.

Strictly speaking, when children grow up, adults who knew them as children should start to address them as вы. In actual practice, it rarely happens—again, the old habit is hard to break.

The general rule of thumb on ты/вы is:

1. with children, always use ты
2. with adults, when in doubt, use вы

As with all social conventions, there are subtleties that need to be taken into consideration: how old is the addressee? Who is speaking to whom?

What to Use and When

Children are never addressed by name and patronymic or вы. These respectful form of address are reserved for adults. Use the child's first name or nickname. Which nickname, you may ask, given that one name can have so many? The answer is simple—use the name that the parents or family friends use, but avoid the more affectionate diminutives (for example, Мишенька, Мишечка) because they convey an affection for and acquaintance with the child that you do not have when you first meet him or her.

Once a person is of college age, вы can be used, but much depends on the situation. (The patronymic, however, is rarely used at this age.) If you yourself are of college age, it is most likely that you will use ты with a contemporary, except in the most formal situations. On the other hand, if you are of the next generation, addressing a college-age person as ты may be deemed inconsiderate, since that individual must address you, the older person, as вы. By using ты, you create an inequality and imply that the other person is still a child. If you are a senior citizen, you are more likely to use ты with a college-age person because of the large age difference. Keep in mind, however, that it is more correct to use вы—no matter how young the person looks, he or she is nevertheless an adult. Furthermore, since the experience of being addressed as вы is new to him or her, the individual will be flattered.

Regardless of your own age, when you address middle-aged people or senior citizens, вы is the most likely choice. If you are younger, you must address middle-aged individuals and senior citizens formally simply *because* you are younger. This generational aspect is important: in situations in which people of the same generation will switch fairly quickly from вы to ты, people of different generations will not. There is always more formality between generations than within them.

It is quite common for middle-aged people and senior citizens to be addressed by name and patronymic and this is the form of address you should use, regardless of your age, unless and until invited to do otherwise. What if you do not know a person's patronymic? Ask —

> Как ваше отчество? or Как вас по отчеству? (What is your patronymic?)

Some Fine (but Essential) Points

Because the name and patronymic are formal, if you use them to address someone, you must also use вы and all related formal pronouns:

> Георгий Петрович, **вы** читали эту книгу? Татьяна Владимировна, **ваш** доклад был очень интересный. (Georgii Petrovich, have you read this book? Tatiana Vladimirovna, your lecture was very interesting.)

The reverse, however, is not always true—if you use вы to address someone, you are not obliged to use the name and patronymic (see the first part of the ты/вы section).

Sometimes the patronymic alone is used to address a person, usually an older person:

Здра́вствуйте, Петро́вич. (Hello, Petrovich.)

Be careful, however: such a form of address lacks the formality of the name and patronymic together, and while its use indicates respect, it also shows affection, closeness, and possibly even playfulness. It usually requires years of friendship to be able to use this term of affectionate respect.

The Parts of Speech

§9.

Nouns

§9.1
WHAT ARE
NOUNS?

Nouns are words that name persons, places, things, or ideas.

§9.2
THE CASE
SYSTEM

To discuss the case system, it is necessary to say a few words about gender and number first. Nouns are masculine, feminine, or neuter in gender. Generally, nouns that refer to male beings are masculine, and those that refer to females are feminine. (There are some exceptions, which will be discussed in §9.3-1.) Not all nouns that refer to inanimate objects (nonliving things) are neuter, however; they may be any gender. How can you tell the gender of a word? By its ending.

Nouns consist of stems and endings. Noun stems end in consonants. Masculine nouns do not have endings, or rather, they are said to have "zero endings." (The zero ending is indicated in charts by the symbol –.) Nouns that end in a consonant are therefore masculine. If the ending is -а or -я, the word is feminine, if -о or -е, neuter. (There are exceptions—see §9.3-1.)

Why are two endings given for each gender? One is the hard ending, the other is the soft ending. How do you know which one to use? As stated earlier, Russian vowels are paired and classified as either hard or soft:

Hard:	а	у	ы	о	э
Soft:	я	ю	и	ё	е

Some case endings such as the ones above come in pairs—one ending has a hard vowel and the other has the corresponding soft vowel. Every noun will take either soft or hard vowel endings, not both.

If, for example, a word ends in -а, you know that it is a hard-stem noun and will take only hard vowel endings in other cases. If a word is a soft-stem noun, it will take only soft vowel endings. Charts of case endings will list both hard and soft endings, so it is only a question of knowing whether a word is a hard-stem or soft-stem noun.

In number, nouns are singular (they refer to one person, place, or thing) or plural (they refer to more than one person, place, or thing). When a noun becomes plural, its ending changes. Generally, feminine nouns and most masculine nouns take an -ы or -и ending. Neuter nouns and some masculine nouns take -а or -я. (Once again, there are exceptions—see §9.3-1.)

The endings given above are the nominative case endings for singular and plural. All nouns have other endings for other cases. Because the case endings vary according to gender and number, you must know a given word's gender and number before trying to determine the appropriate case ending.

Why are there case endings? What is their function? In order to understand the necessity of case in Russian, it is worthwhile to make a brief comparison with English. In any language, sentences are composed of words, but these words are not randomly piled together—they are organized in some way. Otherwise, it would be impossible to know the relationship between them. In English, word order tells us the relationship between the words in the sentence: Jack threw the ball to Mike; Mike threw the ball to Jack. The words are moved to indicate the change in their function, but their form does not change. In Russian, the form of the words changes and the word order may or may not change:

> Сергей бросил мяч Коле; Сергею бросил мяч Коля. (Sergei threw the ball to Kolya; Kolya threw the ball to Sergei.)

A number of other combinations are also possible, including the one most familiar to English speakers:

> Коля бросил мяч Сергею. (Kolya threw the ball to Sergei.)

The word order is very flexible because of the case endings: no matter where you put a word, its ending will tell you the part it plays in the sentence. (In English, only pronouns change their form: I saw him; he saw me.)

There are six cases in Russian. Each of the three genders has its own set of endings for all six cases. This is true for both the singular and the plural, with the result that every word potentially has12 different endings. There is, however, a considerable amount of overlap—some case endings apply to more than one case or to more than one gender. How, then, can you avoid confusing some cases? The context of the sentence will make clear which case is being used.

A noun's declension—that is, the full set of case endings—must be memorized. Because each gender follows certain declensional patterns, however, it is only necessary to memorize several patterns (and, of course, the exceptions). You must be able to decline words (change case endings) and to identify case endings. Otherwise, you will be unable to indicate the function of a word in a sentence that you write, or to recognize a word's function in a sentence that you read or hear.

Following is a list of case names and their primary functions. Keep in mind that this list indicates only the main function of each case: for a more detailed description of the function, see §9.3. All the cases except the nominative are used with certain prepositions, in addition to performing the functions listed below.

1. *Nominative case*—indicates the subject of a sentence.
2. *Accusative case*—indicates the direct object of a sentence.
3. *Genitive case*—indicates possession.
4. *Prepositional case*—refers to the location of someone or something.
5. *Dative case*—indicates the indirect object of a sentence.
6. *Instrumental case*—refers to the instrument, means, or manner by which something is done.

Obviously, since a word can perform only one function at a time, it can have only one case ending at a time. When declining a word, remove any ending that may be present, then add the new ending.

шко́ла—школ + а—школ-   [school]

(-a is the nominative singular ending for hard-stem feminine nouns)

школ + ы—шко́лы   [schools]

(-ы is the nominative plural ending for hard-stem feminine nouns)

Nouns are not the only words that change form—adjectives and pronouns are declined as well. The endings are different from those used for nouns, but, like noun endings, they also depend on gender and number. See §10 on adjectives and §11 on pronouns.

Some masculine nouns whose final stem vowel is -o-, -e-, or -ё- lose that vowel in all cases except the nominative singular: оте́ц—отцу́ [father]. This vowel is called a fleeting vowel. In addition, if -е- or -ё- comes after л-, then a soft sign is added: лёд—льду [ice].

The feminine nouns церковь and любовь [church; love] also have fleeting vowels in all cases of the singular except the nominative, accusative, and instrumental: церкви, любви. Церковь has a fleeting vowel in all cases of the plural as well (любовь has no plural forms). See the appendix for a full chart on these words.

Sometimes the stress shifts in a word when its case or number changes (двери—дверей [doors]). A good dictionary will list the changes in stress.

§9.3
THE CASES

§9.3-1
NOMINA-
TIVE CASE

The nominative case endings for nouns are:

	Masculine	Neuter	Feminine	Feminine
Sing.	—	-о / -е / -ё	-а / -я	—
Plur.	-ы / -и (-а / -я)	-а / -я	-ы / -и	-и

The symbol — stands for "zero ending": nothing is added to the stem of the word. Endings given in parentheses are encountered less frequently. -О/-е/-ё is really one ending, -о, which has a soft variant, -е, and a soft stressed variant, -ё. Similarly, -а/-я is one ending — -а is the hard variant, -я the soft, and -ы/-и is one ending as well — -ы is hard, -и is soft. (The -и ending is, of course, also used when the spelling rules apply.) Consequently, there are not as many endings as it seems.

You learn the nominative singular ending for a noun when you learn the word itself—nouns are listed in glossaries and dictionaries in the nominative singular form (except in the case of nouns that exist only in plural form—they are listed in the nominative plural).

Generally, nouns that have a zero ending are masculine. The last letter of such words will be a consonant. Remember that й, unlike и, is a consonant—words like музей and герой (museum; hero) are masculine. In some masculine words, the last letter is the soft sign, ь. Of course, the soft sign is neither a consonant nor a vowel, but merely a marker of softness. The letter immediately preceding it is always a consonant, however, and as a result—since the soft sign is just a marker—all such words end in a consonant.

When the last letter of a word is a soft sign, determining gender is more difficult. Although some nouns with a soft sign at the end are masculine, others are feminine. (See above chart: feminine nouns that take a zero ending end in a soft sign.) Unfortunately, there is no simple rule for determining whether a noun that ends in a soft sign is masculine or feminine. A few rules of thumb do help:

1. Most nouns that end in -тель or -арь are *masculine* (exceptions—метёль [snowstorm], артёль [crafts cooperative]).

2. The names of the months are *masculine.*

3. Nouns that end in -ость or -есть are *feminine.*

4. Nouns that end in -жь, -чь, -шь, or -щь are *feminine.*

5. Most abstract nouns are *feminine* (жизнь [life], любовь [love]).

For the most part, however, the gender of a word ending in a soft sign has to be memorized when the word itself is learned. Dictionaries and glossaries will indicate whether a word is masculine (*m.*) or feminine (*f.*). In addition, charts may be useful: Pulkina, in *Russian* (Progress Publishers), provides a list of the most common masculine and feminine nouns that end in a soft sign (pp. 28–30).

It is worth adding a note here about the word путь (journey, path). Although it is masculine, it takes a masculine ending only in the instrumental singular (путём). In all other cases, singular and plural, it takes the same endings as feminine nouns with -ь endings:

Singular		**Plural**	
Nom.	путь	**Nom.**	пути
Acc.	путь	**Acc.**	пути
Gen.	пути	**Gen.**	путéй
Prep.	пути	**Prep.**	путях
Dat.	пути	**Dat.**	путям
Inst.	путём	**Inst.**	путями

Some masculine nouns have a fleeting vowel, but it is present only in the nominative singular: отéц (nominative singular)—отцы́ (nominative plural) (father/s); день (nominative singular)—дни (nominative plural) (day/s).

Most neuter nouns end in -о/-е/-ё, but a small number end in -мя. These nouns have their own special declension (see appendix). Fortunately, there are only 10 such nouns, and only a few of them are used frequently: имя (name), знамя (banner), время (time).

Most feminine nouns take the -а/-я ending, but some have a zero ending. All feminine nouns with the zero ending have a soft sign following the final consonant of the word.

It often happens that masculine and neuter endings are identical in a particular case. In the nominative plural, however, it is the masculine and feminine endings that are the same: both are -ы/-и. (Feminine nouns that have a zero ending in the nominative singular always end in -и in the nominative plural. They have a soft stem—they all end with a soft sign in the singular—and therefore take the soft ending in the nominative plural.) Some masculine nouns, however, take the -а/-я ending in the nominative plural—in other words, they take the same ending as do the neuter plural nouns. Over time, the number of masculine nouns taking this ending has increased. (If you read texts from the nineteenth century, you will come across the -ы/-и ending in words that now take -а/-я.) For these nouns, the stress always moves to the ending in the nominative plural (берег — берега [shore/s]). A good dictionary or glossary will indicate which masculine nouns take the -а/-я nominative plural ending by listing "pl. -а" or "pl. -я" after the word.

Special Situations

A handful of masculine nouns, a large number of male nicknames, and a few male full names end in -а/-я in the nominative singular. For example:

> дедушка (grandfather)
> дядя (uncle)
> мужчина (man)
> глава (head [of government, organization, etc.])
> судья (judge)
> Петя, Саша, Никита, Илья

They take the same endings as the -а/-я feminine nouns in all cases, but because these words are masculine, they take masculine adjectives and masculine past tense verb forms. In addition, they are replaced by masculine pronouns.

Some nouns that end in -а change their gender. When they refer to a male, they are masculine; when they refer to a female, they are feminine:

плákса (crybaby)
пья́ница (drunkard)
сирота́ (orphan)
уби́йца (murderer)
у́мница (smart or clever person)
неря́ха (messy person)

When feminine, they take feminine adjectives and past tense verb forms and are replaced by feminine pronouns. When masculine, the adjectives, past tense verb forms, and replacing pronouns are masculine.

Nouns that name professions are often masculine. They do not change their form or gender when they refer to women. These nouns always take masculine adjectives, but the past tense verb forms are feminine when the nouns refer to women, and the pronouns that replace the nouns are feminine:

> Профе́ссор Петро́ва чита́ла докла́д. (Professor Petrova read a lecture.)
> Она́ о́пытный до́ктор. (She's an experienced doctor.)

The same rules apply to nonprofessional terms that are always masculine, such as челове́к (person) and това́рищ (comrade).

Note that words like профе́ссорша and до́кторша, strictly speaking, do not refer to female professionals, but to wives of professionals. In an attempt to use a feminine noun for women in these lines of work, however, some people use this form. This problem arises from the fact that women historically did not work in these professions and only the male term was needed. Секрета́рша (secretary), on the other hand, does mean female secretary.

Indeclinable Nouns

Some nouns that originally came into Russian from other languages do not change their endings at all for any case, singular or plural. This category consists of nouns of foreign origin that end in a vowel (except those that end in -a/-я). With the exception of ко́фе (coffee), which is masculine, those that refer to inanimate objects are neuter:

кафе́ (cafe)
метро́ (metro, subway)
такси́ (taxi)
пальто́ (coat)

Those that are animate are masculine, unless they refer to females, in which case they are feminine. Кенгуру́ (kangaroo), for example, is masculine, unless you are specifically referring to a female kangaroo. Then it is feminine.

Adjectives that are used with indeclinable nouns do change their case endings.

Exceptions and Special Endings

Nouns that have the endings -анин / -янин and -онок / -ёнок in the nominative singular are irregular and have their own declensions (see the appendix for a full chart). In the nominative plural they have the following forms:

англича́нин — англича́не	Englishman/English people
котёнок — котя́та	kitten/s

A small number of masculine and neuter nouns have the following stem change in the plural. Their endings, however, are regular in the nominative and in the other cases.

брат — бра́тья	brother/s
муж — мужья́	husband/s
лист — ли́стья	leaf/leaves
стул — сту́лья	chair/s
[cf.: стол — столы́ (table/s)]	
перо́ — пе́рья	feather/s
крыло́ — кры́лья	wing/s
де́рево — дере́вья	tree/s

Other nouns of this type experience additional changes:

друг — друзья́	friend/s
сын — сыновья́	son/s

The masculine nouns сосе́д and чёрт (neighbor; devil), although hard in the singular, are soft in all cases of the plural. In the nominative plural, they take -и.

There are other words that have irregular endings or forms in the nominative plural:

ребёнок — де́ти	child/children
челове́к — лю́ди	person/people
господи́н — господа́	gentleman/ladies and gentlemen
хозя́ин — хозя́ева	host/s
цвето́к — цветы́	flower/s
не́бо — небеса́	sky/heavens
чу́до — чудеса́	miracle/s
у́хо — у́ши	ear/s
плечо́ — пле́чи	shoulder/s
коле́но — коле́ни	knee/s
я́блоко — я́блоки	apple/s
ку́рица — ку́ры	hen/s
и́мя — имена́	name/s
мать — ма́тери	mother/s
дочь — до́чери	daughter/s

Note that except for плечо́, коле́но, and я́блоко, all the words have a change in the stem. This change persists through all the cases of the plural of these words. In the case of мать, дочь, and имя, the expanded stem is used in all cases, singular and plural, except the nominative and accusative singular (see appendix).

Finally, some words exist only in the singular or only in the plural. They will be marked as such in dictionaries and glossaries. Some of the more common words are listed below:

Singular Only

ABSTRACTIONS

любо́вь (love)
внима́ние (attention)
темнота́ (darkness)
ста́рость (old age)

COLLECTIVES

челове́чество (humanity)
молодёжь (youth)
ме́бель (furniture)
оде́жда (clothing)

SUBSTANCES

серебро́ (silver)
зо́лото (gold)
желе́зо (iron)
мя́со (meat)
карто́фель (potatoes)
молоко́ (milk)
мука́ (flour) [not to be confused with му́ка (torment), which does have
    a plural, му́ки (torments)]

Plural Only

очки́ (glasses)
брю́ки (pants)
но́жницы (scissors)
кавы́чки (quotation marks)
ско́бки (parentheses)
вы́боры (elections)
часы́ (clock, watch)
де́ньги (money)
духи́ (perfume)
су́мерки (dusk)
су́тки (24-hour period)
кани́кулы (school vacation)
ро́ды (childbirth)
имени́ны (saint's day)
по́хороны (funeral)
щи (cabbage soup)
макаро́ны (macaroni)
сли́вки (cream)

The nominative case answers the questions кто? or что? (who? or what?) and has the following functions:

1. It indicates the **subject** of a sentence:

Свéта читáет кни́гу. (Sveta is reading a book.)
Автомоби́ль стои́т на углу́. (The car is standing on the corner.)

2. It is used as the **predicate** in a sentence in which the verb is understood but not written. This is called the predicate nominative:

Ми́ша **хи́мик**. (Misha is a chemist.)
Онá **студéнтка**. (She's a student.)

§9.3-2 ACCUSATIVE CASE

The accusative case endings for nouns are:

	Masculine	**Neuter**	**Feminine** -а/-я	**Feminine** -ь
Sing.	inanimate nouns—like nom. / animate nouns—like gen.	like nom.	-у / -ю	like nom.
Plur.	inanimate nouns—like nom.; animate nouns—like gen.			

-У/-ю is really one ending, -у, with a soft variant, -ю. -у is used for hard-stem nouns, while -ю is used for soft-stem nouns.

The accusative case is somewhat unusual—the -у/-ю feminine ending is the only ending that is not taken either from the nominative or the genitive cases. The other endings are not listed here, since they can be found in §9.3-1 (nominative case) and §9.3-3 (genitive case). The accusative case is also unusual because of the distinction that must be made between animate and inanimate nouns (this distinction is made in the masculine singular and in all the genders of the plural). In no other case is this necessary. Inanimate nouns refer to things or concepts; animate nouns refer to people or animals. Words that designate groups of people or animals, however, are treated as inanimate: for example, нарóд (nation, people), отря́д (military detachment), класс (class).

The accusative case answers the questions когó? что? кудá? (whom? what? where to?) It has the following functions:

1. It is used to indicate the **direct object** in a sentence:

Максим стро́ит **дом**. (Maksim is building a house.)
Со́ня чита́ет **газе́ту**. (Sonia is reading the paper.)

2. It is used in **some expressions of time** to indicate the length of time that an action lasts or to indicate the repetition of an action:

Они́ жи́ли в Пари́же **год**. (They lived in Paris for a year.)
Я хожу́ в магази́н **ка́ждый день**. (I go to the store every day.)

However, when numbers other than one and its compounds (21, 31, etc.) must be used ("two years," "five days," etc.), then the noun following the number must be in the genitive case. See §14 on numbers for an explanation of this problem.

3. The accusative is also used to denote **certain measurements**, such as cost, weight, and distance:

Кни́га сто́ит **рубль**. (The book costs a ruble.)
Арбу́з ве́сит **килогра́мм**. (The watermelon weighs one kilo.)
Мы прошли́ **ми́лю**. (We walked a mile.)

As in #2, above, the introduction of numbers other than one and its compounds into such sentences will require the use of the genitive case in place of the accusative. See §14 on numbers.

Prepositions That Take the Accusative

When used in the following meanings, these prepositions take the accusative:

в   in(to), to, on (in time expressions), at (in time expressions)

> Пе́тя положи́л игру́шки в шкаф. (Petya put the toys in the closet.)
> Я пойду́ в магази́н. (I'll go to the store.)
> Са́ша прие́хала в четве́рг. (Sasha arrived on Thursday.)
> Она́ прие́хала в час. (She arrived at one o'clock.)

на   on(to), to, for (in time expressions)

> Пе́тя положи́л игру́шки на стол. (Petya put the toys on the table.)
> Я пойду́ на по́чту. (I'll go to the post office.)
> Са́ша прие́хала на неде́лю. (Sasha came to stay for a week.)

за   behind, beyond, (in exchange) for, within (in time expressions)

Пётя положи́л игру́шки за дверь. (Petya put the toys behind the door.)

Пти́цы полете́ли за го́ры. (The birds flew beyond the mountains.)

Я ему́ дала́ рубль за кни́гу. (I gave him a ruble [in exchange] for the book.)

Они́ бо́рются за свобо́ду. (They are fighting for freedom.)

Са́ша прие́хала за час. (Sasha got here within an hour.)

под   under

Пётя положи́л игру́шки под крова́ть. (Petya put the toys under the bed.)

через   through, across, in (in time expressions)

Мы идём че́рез парк. (We are walking through the park.)

Мы идём че́рез у́лицу. (We are walking across the street.)

Са́ша уе́дет че́рез неде́лю. (Sasha will leave in a week.)

Мы разгова́ривали че́рез перево́дчика. (We spoke through a translator.)

Note that в and на can also take the prepositional case (see §9.3-4) and that за and под can also take the instrumental case (see §9.3-6). В, на, за, and под take the accusative case when they denote direction—where someone is going, where something is being placed. When these prepositions denote location (where someone or something is located), they take other cases: в and на take the prepositional, and за and под take the instrumental. For example:

Я иду́ в библиоте́ку. / Я чита́ю в библиоте́ке. (I'm going to the library./ I'm reading in the library.)

Он положи́л кни́гу на стол. / Кни́га лежи́т на столе́. (He put the book on the table./ The book is lying on the table.)

Ребёнок побежа́л за де́рево. / Ребёнок сиди́т за де́ревом. (The child ran behind the tree./ The child is sitting behind the tree.)

Мяч покати́лся под крова́ть. / Мяч лежи́т под крова́тью. (The ball rolled under the bed./ The ball is lying under the bed.)

One other question arises in connection with в and на. Since в and на both mean "to," how do you know which to use? It helps to keep their other meanings in mind: в—into, на—onto. Generally speaking, в is used in reference to entering enclosed spaces:

Я иду́ в магази́н, в шко́лу. (I'm going to the store, to school.)

На is used for open spaces:

Я иду́ на пляж, на у́лицу. (I'm going to the beach, outside [out on the street].)

There are exceptions, however. Events generally take на:

Я иду́ на ле́кцию, на конце́рт. (I'm going to a lecture, to a concert.)

Some exceptions are arbitrary: why is it я идý на пóчту (I'm going to the post office) and я идý в парк (I'm going to the park)? In such instances, you have to memorize the appropriate preposition along with the word. For example:

на завóд	to the factory
на стáнцию	to the station
на аэродрóм	to the airport
на Кавкáз	to the Caucasus
в кинó	to the movies
в теáтр	to the theater
в óтпуск	on vacation
в Москвý	to Moscow

Some verbs must be followed by в or на plus the accusative when used in the following meanings:

(рас)сердúться на	to be angry at
кричáть на / крúкнуть на	to yell at
(по)жáловаться на	to complain about
нападáть на / напáсть на	to attack
влия́ть на	to influence, affect
надéяться на	to hope for or rely upon
(по)вéрить в	to believe in
превращáться в / превратúться в	to become
игрáть в	to play [a stated game]

Keep in mind that all the verbs listed above require either в or на. The two prepositions are not interchangeable: you must use the preposition given with the listed word.

Additional Uses of the Listed Prepositions

As noted earlier, в and на are used in some time expressions. There are a few additional time expressions in which these prepositions are used. They are encountered less frequently, but are worth mentioning:

Раз в недéлю я хожý в библиотéку. (Once a week, I go to the library.)
На слéдующий день, Úгорь написáл письмó. (The next day, Igor wrote the letter.)
Он **на год стáрше** меня. (He's a year older than I am.)
Онú жúли в Москвé **в гóды войны́.** (They lived in Moscow during the war years.)
Мы приéхали на дáчу **на день рáньше.** (We arrived at the dacha a day early.)
[This last sentence should not be confused with Мы приéхали на дáчу на день (We came to the dacha for a day).]

Another time expression uses the preposition под:

Под Нóвый Год вся семья́ поéхала к бáбушке. (On New Year's Eve the whole family went to Grandmother's house.)

Под is also used in other types of expressions. It can be used to indicate something, usually a sound, that accompanies an action:

Он заснýл **под шум** телевúзора. (He fell asleep to the sound of the television.)

In addition, it can mean "just under" in reference to age:

Ей ужé **под шестьдесят**. (She's already close to sixty.)

За can be used with the following verbs to indicate getting down to a task:

Нáдо брáться **за рабóту**. (It's necessary to get to work.)
Он принялся **за дéло**.   (He applied himself to the task.)

На can be used in another work-related expression:

На эту рабóту нáдо пять часóв. (This work will take five hours.)

§9.3-3 GENITIVE CASE

The genitive case endings for nouns are:

	Masculine	**Neuter**	**Feminine -а/-я**	**Feminine -ь**
Sing.	-а/-я	-а/-я	-ы / -и	-и
Plur.	-ов / -ев / -ёв -ей [-ь nouns and ж, ч, ш, and щ nouns]	–	–	-ей

The symbol - stands for "zero ending." Words that take a zero ending consist of the stem of the word only.

Words that end in -мя have their own special declension (although they do take a zero ending in the genitive plural, as do other neuters). See the appendix for a complete chart.

The -а/-я ending is really one ending, -а, with a soft variant, -я. The same is true of the -ы/-и and -ов/-ев endings (and -ёв is just the soft stressed variant). Use the hard variants for hard-stem nouns, the soft variants for soft-stem nouns. Use -ёв when the stress falls on the ending in -ев nouns. (The -и and -ей endings are soft and have no hard variants.)

Nouns with a zero ending will be hard or soft, depending on whether the stem of the word itself is hard or soft.

Remember that, as always, the spelling rules apply for all endings.

Genitive plural endings are considered notoriously difficult, but as you can see from the above chart, they are really fairly straightforward. Most masculines take -ов/-ев/-ёв, neuters and -а/-я feminines generally take a zero ending, and feminines ending in -ь have the -ей ending. Of course, the plural is simpler for the other cases: in three of the cases, there is only one ending for all genders. Nevertheless, the genitive plural is not hopelessly difficult: as a rule of thumb, keep in mind that the endings given above are used most often.

For the masculine, the less frequently encountered genitive plural ending is -ей. It is used for all masculines ending in the soft sign or ж, ч, ш, or щ:

автомобиль — автомобилей	car/s
нож — ножей	knife/knives
врач — врачей	doctor/s

(Because they are soft in the plural, the nouns сосе́д and чёрт [neighbor; devil] take this ending as well—сосе́дей, черте́й.)

The zero ending is not one of the expected endings for masculines in the genitive plural, but it is taken by a handful of nouns. The most common are:

раз	time [as in number of times something is done]
глаз	eye
во́лос	a hair
солда́т	soldier
сапо́г	boot
боти́нок	shoe

Челове́к (person/s) is also used as a special genitive plural instead of люде́й (people) in certain situations (see below).

As you would expect, given their soft stems in the plural, nouns of the type брат/бра́тья take -ев in the genitive plural. For example:

бра́тья — бра́тьев	brothers
сту́лья — сту́льев	chairs

Note, however, that there are exceptions:

сыновья́ — сынове́й	sons
друзья́ — друзе́й	friends
мужья́ — муже́й	husbands

Nouns ending in -анин / -янин and -онок / -ёнок in the nominative singular have irregular genitive plural forms:

граждани́н — гра́ждан	citizen/s
армяни́н — армя́н	Armenian/s
цыплёнок — цыпля́т	chick/s
медвежо́нок — медвежа́т	bear cub/s

See the appendix for the full charts of these types of nouns.

Neuter nouns generally take a zero ending in the genitive plural, but nouns that end in -ие seem to be an exception: (зда́ние — зда́ний) (building/s). However, this ending is also a zero ending. It is just more difficult to see that this is so:

zdanije → genitive plural zero ending → *zdanije - e = zdanij*

Once the final vowel is removed to create the zero ending, the -j must be represented by -й (because it is preceded by a vowel). As a result, you get зда́ний.

Neuter nouns that end in -o in the nominative singular *and* -ья in the nominative plural take -ьев in the genitive plural. For example:

Nom. Singular	Nom. Plural	Gen. Plural
де́рево	дере́вья	дере́вьев (tree/s)
крыло́	кры́лья	кры́льев (wing/s)

Пла́тье (gen. plural пла́тьев) (dress/es) also takes this ending. (Note that a small number of masculine nouns do the same: see above.)

The following neuter nouns are also irregular in the genitive plural:

мо́ре — море́й	sea/s
по́ле — поле́й	field/s
у́хо — уше́й	ear/s
плечо́ — плече́й	shoulder/s

There are two neuter nouns that take the -ов ending instead of a zero ending in the genitive plural:

о́блако — облако́в (cloud/s), су́дно — судо́в (boat, ship) (Note the additional change in the stem of the latter word.)

Feminine nouns in -а/-я generally have a zero ending in the genitive plural, but feminines that end in -ия (or -ея), like neuters that end in -ие, seem to be an exception to this rule (лаборато́рия — лаборато́рий [lab/s], иде́я — иде́й [idea/s]). These endings, however, are zero endings, just as the neuter ending (зда́ние — зда́ний) is a zero ending (see above).

laboratorija → gen. plural zero ending → *laboratorija - a = laboratorij*
ideja → gen. plural zero ending → *ideja - a = idej*

Once you remove the final vowel to create the zero ending, the -j must be represented as -й (because it is preceded by a vowel). As a result, you get лаборато́рий, иде́й.
(Remember that although иде́й appears to have a -ей ending, it does not. The -ей is part of the stem.)

The same is true for a small number of feminine nouns that end in -ья. Статья́ (article), for example, goes through the following changes in the formation of the genitive plural:

stat'ja → gen. plural zero ending → *stat'ja - a*

In addition, there is an inserted vowel — -e, not -o, in this case because of the softness:

stat/e/j (стате́й)

Судья́ (суде́й) (judge/s), семья́ (семе́й) (family/families), and свинья́ (свине́й) (pig/s) follow the same pattern.
(The neuter noun ружьё [rifle] goes through a similar process:

ruz'jo → gen. pl. zero ending → *ruz'jo - o* → inserted vowel → *ruz/e/j*

Hence, ру́жей.)

Again, all the above words have a zero ending, although it may not be apparent at first glance.

Some Potential Troublespots

When forming the genitive plural of masculine nouns that end in -й, remember not to preserve the -й: it is represented in the soft ending (геро́й — геро́ев [hero/heroes]).

When forming the genitive plural of nouns that end in -ь, remember not to preserve the -ь: it is represented in the soft ending (дверь — двере́й [door/s]).

Note also that all words ending in -ь, whether masculine or feminine, take the same ending in the genitive plural.

When forming the genitive plural for -я feminine nouns, remember that, while the ending is dropped, the softness must remain:

nedelja → gen. plural zero ending → *nedelja - a*

Here, because j is preceded by a consonant, it is represented by the soft sign: неде́ль (weeks). There are some exceptions; most words that end in -ня have a hard ending in the genitive plural (пе́сня — пе́сен [song/s], ви́шня — ви́шен [cherry/cherries]).

Inserted Vowels

When a word has a zero ending and the stem ends in a consonant cluster, a vowel (o or e) is inserted between the consonants. (However, the consonant clusters ст, зд, and ств are exceptions: for example, звёзд [stars]. The words ка́рта [map] and ла́мпа [lamp] are also exceptions to this rule.)

Feminines that end in a consonant + ка in the nominative singular (but where the consonant is *not* ж, ч, ш, щ, or й) have o as the inserted vowel. In other situations, e is generally used.

Note the following:

письмо́ — пи́сем	letter/s
копе́йка — копе́ек	kopeck/s

The soft sign and the -й are not written in the genitive plural because they are contained in the softness of the inserted vowel e.

Words That Exist Only in the Plural

Words that exist only in the plural take one of several endings in the genitive plural. The genitive plural endings for these words must be memorized.

Zero Ending

брю́ки — брюк	pants
но́жницы — но́жниц	scissors
макаро́ны — макаро́н	macaroni
кани́кулы — кани́кул	school vacation
имени́ны — имени́н	saint's day
по́хороны — похоро́н	funeral
ша́хматы — ша́хмат	chess
хло́поты — хлопо́т	trouble, bother

The following words take the zero ending with an inserted vowel:

де́ньги — де́нег	money
сли́вки — сли́вок	cream
кавы́чки — кавы́чек	quotation marks
ско́бки — ско́бок	parentheses
су́тки — су́ток	24-hour period

-ов Ending

очки́ — очко́в	glasses
часы́ — часо́в	clock, watch
духи́ — духо́в	perfume

вы́боры — вы́боров	elections
ро́ды — ро́дов	childbirth

-ей ending

де́ти — дете́й	children
лю́ди — люде́й	people
щи — щей	cabbage soup

The Special Genitive Ending -у/-ю

Finally, there is a special genitive ending, -у/-ю, that is sometimes used with some masculine nouns. It is called the partitive genitive because it is used to indicate some part of a substance.

чай — ча́ю	tea
са́хар — са́хару	sugar
суп — су́пу	soup
сыр — сы́ру	cheese
лук — лу́ку	onion
рис — ри́су	rice
снег — сне́гу	snow
песо́к — песку́	sand
бензи́н — бензи́ну	gasoline
наро́д — наро́ду	nation, people

For example:

Я хочу́ ча́ю. (I would like some tea.)

The use of the partitive genitive is limited, however. It cannot be used if:

1. you do not mean "some" but are referring to the substance in general,
2. you use an adjective to modify the word, or
3. you negate the sentence.

How do you know which masculine nouns take this special ending? A good dictionary will list the ending following any word in this category. Check the explanatory material at the beginning of the dictionary to see whether, and how, it is listed. Note: хлеб (bread) does not have a partitive genitive.

The genitive case answers the questions кого? чего? чей? (whose? of what?) It has the following functions:

1. It indicates **possession**:

Это журна́л **моего́ профе́ссора**. (This is my professor's magazine.)
Мы прие́хали на автомоби́ле **мое́й сестры́**. (We came in my sister's car.)

The person who possesses something is expressed by the genitive. Word order is very strict here—the thing possessed has to come *before* the person who possesses it.

This is the opposite of the word order in English: We came in *my sister's car*.

2. The genitive is used in sentences that require **"of"** in English:

> Дети поломáли рýчку **двери**. (The children broke the handle of the door.)
> Дирéктор **завóда** говори́т с рабóчими. (The director of the factory is speaking with the workers.)
> Онá жéнщина **твёрдого харáктера**. (She's a woman of strong character.)
> Мы занимáемся изучéнием **э́того вопрóса**. (We are occupied with the study of this question.)
> Емý не нрáвится шум **гóрода**. (He doesn't like the noise of the city.)
> Чтéние **доклáдчика** дли́лось два часá. (The presentation of the lecturer went on for two hours.)

Some of the above sentences can also be translated into English by using *'s*: The lecturer's presentation went on for two hours.

3. The genitive case follows words of **measure and quantity**. The genitive singular is used for substances, the genitive plural for discrete items that can be counted.

> мнóго дéнег (a lot of money)
> мáло врéмени (little time, insufficient time)
> скóлько рабóты? (how much work?)
> нéсколько студéнтов (several students)

Keep in mind that sentences with such constructions usually require a neuter singular verb in the past and a third-person singular verb in the nonpast:

> Нéсколько **книг** лежáло (лежи́т) на столé. (Several books were [are] lying on the table.)
> [Compare: Кни́ги лежáли (лежáт) на столé. (The books were [are] lying on the table.)]

This does not occur, however, when the subject of the sentence is unaffected by the word of measure or quantity (that is, when the word of measure or quantity applies to some word other than the subject):

> Мы купи́ли (кýпим) кило́ мáсла. (We bought [will buy] a kilo of butter.)

The special genitive plural человéк (persons) is used with скóлько, нéсколько (how much, several), and numbers (see below); with other words of measure and quantity, use the genitive plural of лю́ди — людéй (people).

4. The genitive case must follow **cardinal numerals** except 1 and its compounds (21, 31, etc., but not 11). Treat 1 and its compounds as you would any other adjectives. (Оди́н declines like э́тот; see §10.5-3.) As for the other numerals: sometimes the genitive singular follows them, sometimes the genitive plural.

Numerals:	Case and Number of the Adjective That Follows:	Case and Number of the Noun That Follows:
2, 3, 4 or their compounds	genitive plural (for feminines— nominative plural also possible)	genitive singular
5-10 or their compounds, and 11-14	genitive plural	genitive plural

Keep in mind, however, that this applies only when the noun affected by the numerals is in the nominative or accusative position in the sentence. In other cases, other rules apply (see §14).

> Я ему далá шесть **стáрых книг**. (I gave him six old books.)
> Трѝдцать два **óпытных врачá** рабóтают в этой больнѝце. (Thirty-two experienced doctors work in this hospital.)

Remember to use the special genitive plural человéк (persons) with numerals that require the genitive plural. Another special genitive plural, лет (years), must also be used in the same situations. But гóда (nominative singular—год [year]) is used when the genitive singular is needed.

5. The genitive can denote "some" of a substance. (As noted above, some masculine nouns have a special partitive ending for this purpose—other nouns take their usual genitive ending.)

> Он выпил **воды** и съел **хлéба**. (He drank some water and ate some bread.)

6. Genitive is always required with нет, нé было, and не бýдет (present tense, past tense, and future tense forms of "not present" or "not existing"). The person or object not present is in the genitive:

> **Áнны** здесь нé было весь день. (Anna wasn't here all day.)
> **Учѝтеля** нет в клáссе. (The teacher is not in the classroom.)
> Compare: Áнна здесь былá весь день. (Anna was here all day.)
> Учѝтель в клáссе. (The teacher is in the classroom.)

Нет, не было, and не бýдет are impersonal constructions, and sentences containing them do not have subjects in the nominative. They are not to be confused with personal constructions that contain negations:

> Я нé была в библиотéке. (I didn't go to the library.)
> Я не купѝла молокó. (I didn't buy the milk.)

7. The genitive is used with **dates** to denote "on":

Мы начали занятия **пятнáдцатого сентября**. (We started classes on
September 15th.)

Adjectives That Take the Genitive Case

пóлный (-ое, -ая, -ые) (full)
   short forms—пóлон, пóлно, полнá, пóлны
достóйный (-ое, -ая, -ые) (worthy)
   short forms—достóин, достóйно, достóйна, достóйны

Ребёнок пóлон **жѝзни**. (The child is full of life.)

The genitive case can also be used with short comparative
adjectives:

Кóшка быстрée собáки. (The cat is faster than the dog.)

(The same comparison can be made without the genitive by
adding чем: Кóшка быстрée, чем собáка. [The cat is faster
than the dog.])

Verbs That Take the Genitive Case

Some commonly used verbs take the genitive case when
used in the following meanings:

пугáться / испугáться	to be frightened (by something)
боя́ться	to be afraid (of something)
стыдѝться	to be ashamed (of something)
добивáться / добѝться	to try to achieve (imperfective aspect) or to achieve (perfective aspect) (something)
достигáть / достѝгнуть	to reach for (imperfective aspect) or to reach (perfective aspect) (something)
касáться / коснýться	to touch (upon something)
желáть	to wish (for something)

Тáня бойтся **собáк**.	Tanya is afraid of dogs.
Рóма испугáлся **грóма**.	Roma was frightened by the thunder.
Учёные добѝлись **результáтов**.	The scientists achieved [got] results.
Он не коснýлся **э́того вопрóса**.	He didn't touch upon that question.

Prepositions That Take the Genitive Case

When used in the following meanings, these prepositions
take the genitive.

óколо	near; approximately (in reference to time)
у	by (in reference to location)
мѝмо	by (in reference to motion)
от	(away) from
из	(out) of; from

из-за	from behind something; because of something
из-под	from under something
с	off; from
до	as far as; before; until
после	after
без	without
кроме	besides; except
против	against; opposite
для	for

Стул стоит у стола. (The chair is standing by the table.)
Он отошёл от окна. (He walked away from the window.)
Зина вышла из комнаты. (Zina came out of the room.)
Мы скоро дошли до дома. (We soon reached the house.)
Я купила молоко для ребёнка. (I bought milk for the child.)

The preposition с can also take the instrumental case (see §9.3-6).

Many of the prepositions used with the genitive denote place, time, or direction (in the sense of where something or someone is coming *from*).

Some of these prepositions also have more complicated uses. The most important is у + the genitive case to express possession:

У меня все книги. (I have all the books [all the books are in my possession].)
У Антона твои деньги. (Anton has your money [your money is in Anton's possession].)

This construction is used far more often than the Russian verb "to have" (иметь), which is, however, used with abstractions: Я имею возможность поехать на юг. (I have an opportunity to go to the south.)

But у + the genitive can also indicate "at someone's home or place of work":

Мы были у Саши. (We were at Sasha's.)
Больной был у врача. (The sick person was at the doctor's.)

Finally, у + the genitive can be used with verbs such as взять to denote taking something away from someone:

Он взял у ребёнка спички. (He took the matches away from the child.)

The preposition от is used in a number of idiomatic expressions:

Врачи ему дали лекарство от боли. (The doctors gave him medicine for the pain.)
Улица была мокрая от дождя. (The street was wet from rain.)
Где ключ от дома? (Where is the key to the house?)

"Есть" vs. "Нет"

As stated above, нет, не было, and не будет require the genitive case. The positive of нет is есть, which is invariable in form and does not require the genitive. Есть, however, has limited uses and is omitted if you do not wish to stress the existence of something, but merely want to mention a feature or quality of that thing. You also do not use it if you are talking about an illness or an emotional state (see §6 for more information).

У меня нет самолёта. (I don't have an airplane.)
У меня есть самолёт. (I have an airplane.)
У меня большой самолёт. (I have a big airplane.)

In positive sentences in the past and future tenses, all six forms of the verb быть are used. Although не было and не будет are invariable, the positive forms of быть agree in gender and number with the subject of the sentence. The subject is in the nominative. In the negative sentences there is no subject in the nominative.

На улице была толпа. (A crowd was in the street.)
На улице не было толпы. (There was no crowd in the street.)
Студенты будут на собрании. (The students will be at the meeting.)
Студентов не будет на собрании. (There will be no students at the meeting.)

The Genitive Case vs. the Accusative Case

As stated in #6 of the functions of the genitive, нет, не было, and не будет are impersonal constructions. They are not to be confused with personal constructions that contain negations: these have their own rules and present their own special difficulties.

If a personal construction has a direct object in the accusative, and that sentence is negated, then the direct object can be in either the accusative or the genitive. The rules for determining which to use are not hard and fast. It is best to learn the guidelines and expect some examples to fall into a gray area in which either case can be used. (Keep in mind that these guidelines apply only when the verb in the sentence takes the accusative in a non-negated sentence. If the verb requires a dative, instrumental, or genitive complement, then the negation of the sentence will not change the case.)

Use the accusative case when:
- the direct object is specific—

Они не купили эту лодку. (They didn't buy that boat.)

- the negation does not apply to the verb—

Не он читал лекции. (He was not the one who gave the lectures.)

The negative particle must immediately precede the verb if it is the verb that is being negated. Further, be careful if an

infinitive appears in the sentence: the negation may apply
to the auxiliary verb. In such a case, you would also use the
accusative.

Use the genitive case when:

• the direct object is abstract, indefinite, or refers to a
category—

Рабо́чие не теря́ют вре́мени. (The workers don't waste time.)

Some verbs, whether they are negated or not, will take
both genitive and accusative. How do you know when to
use which? Again, use the accusative if the object is specific, and the genitive if the object is abstract, indefinite, or
refers to a category.

хоте́ть	to want
проси́ть	to ask
тре́бовать	to demand
ждать	to wait
иска́ть	to look for

Я жду **Ма́шу**. (I'm waiting for Masha.) [accusative]
Он тре́бует **внима́ния**. (He's demanding attention.) [genitive]

§9.3-4 PREPOSI-TIONAL CASE

The prepositional case endings for nouns are:

	Masculine	Neuter	Feminine -а/-я	Feminine -ь
Sing.	-е (-и) [for -ий masc. nouns]	-е (-и) [for -ие neuter nouns]	-е (-и) [for -ия fem. nouns]	-и
Plur.	-ах/-ях			

-Ах/-ях is really one ending: -ах is the hard variant, -ях
is the soft variant. Use the hard one for hard-stem nouns,
the soft one for soft stems.

Remember that, as always, the spelling rules apply.

As you can see from the above chart, the prepositional
case is a fairly easy one. The only irregular ending is -и:

ге́ний — ге́нии	genius
зда́ние — зда́нии	building
ста́нция — ста́нции	station

The same ending is also used with all feminines ending in a
soft sign: ло́шадь — ло́шади (horse). But remember that the
vast majority of nouns take -е in the prepositional singular.

Exceptions

Words ending in -анин/-янин and -онок/-ёнок take the standard prepositional endings, but, as always for these words, the stem is changed in the plural:

англича́нине — англича́нах	Englishman/English people
котёнке — котя́тах	kitten/s

Note the fleeting vowel in the prepositional singular of котёнок. The vowel will fall out in the prepositional singular of all words ending in -онок/-ёнок.

The words брат, друг, муж, сын, стул, and лист are not irregular, but they have a stem change in their plural form. They take the soft ending in the prepositional plural:

бра́те — бра́тьях	brother/s
дру́ге — друзья́х	friend/s
му́же — мужья́х	husband/s
сы́не — сыновья́х	son/s
сту́ле — сту́льях	chair/s
листе́ — ли́стьях	leaf/leaves

Note the consonant mutation in друзья́х and the expanded stem in сыновья́х.

The nouns сосе́д and чёрт (neighbor; devil) are soft in the plural and therefore take the soft variant in the prepositional plural.

In the neuter, the irregular -мя nouns take -и in the prepositional singular (и́мени [name]) and a hard ending in the prepositional plural (имена́х).

Де́рево (tree) takes the same prepositional plural ending as masculine words like брат: дере́вьях.

In the feminine, the nouns мать and дочь (mother; daughter) take the expected prepositional endings, but remember that you must use the expanded stem in both the singular and the plural: ма́тери — матеря́х.

The feminine noun це́рковь (church), which is ordinarily soft, takes a hard ending in the prepositional plural: церква́х (see appendix).

Some masculine nouns sometimes take a special -у/-ю prepositional ending aside from the standard ending. The special ending can be used only if the preposition preceding the word is в or на. In addition, it generally is used only when reference is being made to a physical location or to time. When the special ending is used, the stress falls on the ending. The most common words that take this ending are:

сад — в саду́	garden
лес — в лесу́	forest
бе́рег — на берегу́	shore
мост — на мосту́	bridge

у́гол — в углу́	corner
пол — на полу́	floor
нос — на носу́	nose
год — в году́	year

How do you know which masculine nouns take this special ending? A good dictionary will list the ending for the relevant words. Check the explanatory material at the beginning of the dictionary to see whether, and how, it is listed. Note: most words that take this ending have only one syllable in the nominative singular.

The prepositional case answers the questions о ком? о чём? где? (about whom? about what? where?) It has the following functions—

1. It indicates **location** (and is therefore sometimes called the locative case):

Я живу́ в го́роде. (I live in the city.)
Библиоте́ка нахо́дится на э́той у́лице. (The library is on this street.)

2. It denotes the **person or thing that is being spoken or thought of**:

Студе́нты говори́ли о му́зыке. (The students were talking about music.)

Prepositions That Take the Prepositional Case

When used in the following meanings, these prepositions take the prepositional.

The prepositional case is different from the other cases because it cannot be used without a preposition (this, of course, explains its name).

в	in
на	on; at
о	about (concerning)
при	under (in reference to time); at, during (in reference to time); connected to or associated with; by; in the presence of

Она́ весь ве́чер рабо́тала в библиоте́ке. (All evening, she worked in the library.)
В де́тстве мы жи́ли в дере́вне. (In childhood we lived in the country.)
Он был в краси́вом костю́ме. (He was in a nice-looking suit.)
Ба́бушка прие́хала в го́род на по́езде. (Grandmother came to the city on the train. [Compare: Ба́бушка прие́хала в го́род по́ездом—Grandmother came to the city by train.])
Мы бы́ли на собра́нии. (We were at the meeting.)
Газе́та лежи́т на сту́ле. (The newspaper is lying on the chair.)
Ди́ма до́лго расска́зывал нам о пое́здке. (Dima told us about the trip at great length.)
При Никола́е II была́ револю́ция. (Under Nicholas II, there was a revolution.)
Я дам ему́ э́ту кни́гу при встре́че. (I'll give him this book when we meet.)
При больни́це есть большо́й сад. (There is a large garden connected to the hospital.)

Мы шли че́рез по́ле при све́те луны́. (We were walking through the field by moonlight.)

Он ничего́ не говори́л при Гри́ше. (He didn't say anything in the presence of Grisha.)

The prepositions в and на can also take the accusative case (see §9.3-2). See §9.3-2 to learn when to use в and на with the prepositional and when to use them with the accusative. The same section also explains which words take в and which take на (the choice is not always obvious). Fortunately, there are no new rules in this regard for the prepositional: if a word takes на in the accusative, it will take it in the prepositional, too. The same applies for в.

Some verbs must be followed by в or на plus the prepositional when used in the following meanings:

говори́ть на	to speak in [a particular language]
писа́ть на	to write in [a particular language]
игра́ть на	to play [an instrument]
уча́ствовать в	to participate in
жени́ться на	to marry
наста́ивать на / настоя́ть на	to insist on
сомнева́ться в	to have doubts (about someone or something)
убежда́ться в / убеди́ться в	to become convinced (of something)
обвиня́ть в / обвини́ть в	to accuse ([someone] of something)
признава́ться в / призна́ться в	to admit (something)

Анто́н хорошо́ игра́ет на роя́ле. (Anton plays the piano well. [Compare: Анто́н хорошо́ **игра́ет в** футбо́л—Anton plays soccer well.])

Он жени́лся на Ма́ше год наза́д. (He married Masha a year ago.)

Учёный призна́лся в оши́бке.   (The scholar admitted his mistake.)

The first two verbs listed above are usually used in questions: На како́м языке́ вы говори́те? (Which language are you speaking?)

Keep in mind that all of the verbs listed above require either в or на. The two prepositions are not interchangeable: you must use the preposition given with the listed word.

§9.3-5 DATIVE CASE

The dative case endings for nouns are:

	Masculine and Neuter	**Feminine** **-а/-я**	**Feminine** **-ь**
Sing.	-у / -ю	-е (-и) [for -ия nouns]	-и
Plur.		-ам / -ям	

-у/-ю is really one ending: -у is the hard variant and -ю the soft variant. The same is true for -ам/-ям. Use the hard variants for hard-stem nouns and the soft variants for soft-stem nouns. Remember that, as always, the spelling rules apply.

Dative case endings present no problems: there are relatively few of them, and there is only one irregular ending, -и for -ия feminine nouns (ста́нция — ста́нции) (station). It is also used with all feminine nouns ending in a soft sign: жизнь — жи́зни (life). Most feminine nouns take the -е ending, however.

Exceptions

Words ending in -анин/-янин and -онок/ ёнок take the standard dative endings, but, as always, the stem is changed in the plural:

граждани́ну — гра́жданам	citizen/s
медвежо́нку — медвежа́там	bear cub/s

Note the fleeting vowel in the dative singular of медвежо́нок. The vowel will fall out in the dative singular of all words ending in -онок/-ёнок.

The words брат, друг, муж, сын, стул, and лист are not irregular, but they have a stem change in their plural form. They take the soft ending in the dative plural:

бра́ту — бра́тьям	brother/s
му́жу — мужья́м	husband/s
дру́гу — друзья́м	friend/s
сы́ну — сыновья́м	son/s
сту́лу — сту́льям	chair/s
листу́ — ли́стьям	leaf/leaves

Note the consonant mutation in друзья́м and the expanded stem in сыновья́м.

The nouns сосе́д and чёрт (neighbor; devil) are soft in the plural and therefore take the soft variant in the dative plural.

Among the neuter nouns, the irregular -мя nouns take -и in the dative singular (и́мени) (name) and a hard ending in the dative plural (имена́м).

Де́рево (tree) takes the same dative plural ending as masculine words like брат: дере́вьям.

Among the feminine nouns, мать and дочь (mother; daughter) take the expected dative endings, but remember that you must use the expanded stem in both the singular and the plural: до́чери — дочеря́м.

The feminine noun це́рковь (church), which is ordinarily soft, takes a hard ending in the dative plural: церква́м (see appendix).

The dative case answers the questions кому́? чему́? (to whom? to what?) It has the following functions:

1. It denotes the **indirect object** of the sentence:

Ми́ша дал я́блоко **А́нне**. (Misha gave the apple to Anna.)

2. It is used in a variety of **impersonal constructions**. In such constructions, there is no subject in the nominative case—the person performing the action (or experiencing some state or condition) is expressed in the dative case. (For more on impersonal expressions, see below.)

Де́тям хо́лодно на у́лице. (The children are cold outside.)
Па́влу хо́чется игра́ть в футбо́л. (Pavel wants to play soccer.)

3. The dative is required when discussing **age**.

Ба́бушке сто лет. (Grandmother is 100 years old.)

Adjectives That Take the Dative Case

благода́рный (-ое, -ая, -ые) (grateful)
   short forms—благода́рен, благода́рно, благода́рна, благода́рны
   (and its negation, неблагода́рный)
ве́рный (-ое, -ая, -ые)   (faithful)
   short forms—ве́рен, ве́рно, верна́, ве́рны
рáд (-о, -а, -ы)   (happy)
   [only the short form of this adjective exists]

Cа́ша был благода́рен **Алёше** за его́ по́мощь. (Sasha was grateful to Alyosha for his help.)
Все ра́ды **прие́зду** Кири́лла. (Everyone is happy about Kirill's arrival.)

Verbs That Take the Dative Case

Some commonly used verbs take the dative case when used in the following meanings:

ра́доваться / обра́доваться	to be happy (about something)
ве́рить / пове́рить	to believe (in something)
доверя́ть / дове́рить	to trust (someone)
помога́ть / помо́чь	to help (someone)
зави́довать / позави́довать	to envy (someone)
изменя́ть / измени́ть	to betray (someone)
отвеча́ть / отве́тить	to answer (someone)
сове́товать / посове́товать	to advise (someone)
звони́ть / позвони́ть	to call (someone) on the telephone
меша́ть / помеша́ть	to interfere (with someone's work)
улыба́ться / улыбну́ться	to smile (at someone)
удивля́ться / удиви́ться	to be surprised (about something)
учи́ться / научи́ться	to study (something)
принадлежа́ть	to belong (to someone or something)

Ты меша́ешь **мне** чита́ть. (You're interfering with my reading.)

Ученики не отвечают **учителю** на вопросы. (The students aren't answering the teacher's questions.)

Эта организация помогает **бедным**. (This organization helps the poor. [See §10.5-7 on substantivized adjectives.])

Я **тебе** советую поехать в Лондон. (I advise you to go to London.)

Рита позвонила **Жене** по телефону. (Rita called Zhenya on the phone.)

Эта книга принадлежит **профессору**. (This book belongs to the professor.)

(If membership in an organization is being expressed, then the preposition к must also be used, as well as the dative: Они больше не принадлежат к коммунистической партии. [They no longer belong to the Communist Party.])

Prepositions That Take the Dative Case

When used in the following meanings, these prepositions take the dative.

(Note that по has quite a wide number of meanings).

по   along; by (means of); around (inside a given space); on; at; in; according to; at a rate of (in reference to single objects); to (separate points or from one point to another); because of; in or on (a particular subject or field)

к   to; toward; by (in reference to time); for

Мы идём по улице и разговариваем. (We're walking along the street and talking.)

Он мне позвонил по телефону и я его сразу узнала по голосу. (He called me on the phone [by means of the phone] and I immediately recognized him by his voice.)

Учёный ходил по комнате и думал об эксперименте. (The scientist walked around the room and thought about the experiment.)

Мяч ударил ребёнка по голове. (The ball hit the child on the head.)

По вторникам и четвергам я хожу на уроки, а по вечерам я работаю. (On Tuesdays and Thursdays I go to class, and in the evenings I work.) [Note: по утрам, по вечерам, по ночам (in the mornings, in the evenings, at night)—but there is no such construction for день (day).]

По моему мнению, надо это сделать по плану. (In my opinion, this should be done according to plan.)

Все дети выпили по бутылке сока. (All the children drank [at a rate of] a bottle of juice each.)

После школы, все ученики разошлись по домам. (After school, all the students went to their homes.)

Мы ходили по магазинам весь день. (All day long we went from store to store.)

Она не пришла на собрание по болезни. (She didn't come to the meeting because of illness.)

Я взяла учебник по химии, а у меня сейчас урок по физике. (I brought my textbook on chemistry, but I have a class in physics right now.)

Он подошёл к окну и посмотрел в сад. (He came up to the window and looked into the garden.)

Дети вернулись домой к ужину. (The children returned home by dinner.)

Хозяйка подала пирог к чаю. (The hostess gave [us] pie for [along with] tea.)

A number of verbs are generally followed by the preposition к. The most common are:

привы́кнуть к	to get used to (something)
приуча́ть к / приучи́ть к	to train [someone] to (do something)
гото́виться к / пригото́виться к	to prepare for (something)
относи́ться к	to treat (someone [well, badly, etc.])

Impersonal Constructions

The dative case is used in a variety of impersonal constructions. These constructions do not have a subject in the nominative: the person performing the action (or experiencing some state or condition) is expressed in the dative case.

1. Impersonal constructions with adverbs

Such constructions may consist of nothing more than an adverb:

Хо́лодно. ([It's] cold.)

An infinitive may be added:

Хо́лодно игра́ть. ([It's too] cold to play.)

The person experiencing the condition may also be added (along with additional information):

Ребёнку хо́лодно игра́ть в саду́. ([It's too] cold for the child to play outside.)

The person experiencing the condition must be in the dative case.

The most common adverbs of this type are:

[Мне]	интере́сно	interesting
	ску́чно	boring
	(не)прия́тно	(un)pleasant
	ве́село	cheerful
	(не)удо́бно	(un)comfortable
	бо́льно	painful
	пло́хо	bad
	хорошо́	good
	легко́	easy
	тру́дно	hard
	хо́лодно	cold
	жа́рко	hot
	жаль	sorry

To form the past and future of these constructions, use бы́ло **and** бу́дет:

Нам бу́дет прия́тно вас ви́деть. (We will be pleased to see you. [(It) will be pleasant for us to see you.])

2. Impersonal constructions with verbs ending in -ся

Some verbs that end in -ся do not take a subject in the nominative. Instead, the actor is in the dative. The most common verbs of this type are:

хотéться   to want
казáться   to seem
Вѝте хóчется поéхать в кинó. (Vitya wants to go to the movies.)
Мне кáжется, что я опоздáю на пóезд. (It seems to me that I will be
   late for the train.)

Казáться is used with что (that) and хотéться requires that
an infinitive follow it. In the nonpast tenses, always use the
third-person singular form of the verb. In the past tense, use
the neuter singular. Since there is no subject in the nominative, the verb has nothing with which to agree, and it therefore takes only these forms.

Казáться can be used only as an impersonal -ся verb,
but this is not true of хотéться:

Вѝтя хóчет поéхать в кинó. (Vitya wants to go to the movies.)

In such sentences, the person is in the nominative instead
of the dative, and the verb agrees with the nominative subject. Is there a difference in meaning between this sentence
and the previous one? When there is a subject in the nominative, it is more "responsible" for the action of the sentence. When the person is in the dative, on the other hand,
he or she is more the "receiver" of the condition than the initiator of it.

Modal Expressions

The dative case is used in a number of modal expressions.

Нáдо / Нýжно / Необходѝмо — it is necessary.

The first two forms are interchangeable; необходѝмо is
stronger and implies that something is essential and
unavoidable. These expressions are used with infinitives.
The person experiencing the condition may also be added,
and will be in the dative case:

Нýжно отдыхáть. (It is necessary to rest.)
Мáрку нáдо занимáться. (Mark needs to study.)
Всем ученикáм необходѝмо прочитáть эту книгу. (All the students
   have to read this book.)

The verb pair приходѝться / прийтѝсь has a similar function and also requires a dative complement:

Марѝне приходѝлось éздить в гóрод кáждую недéлю. (Marina had
   to go into the city every week.)

Мóжно / Нельзя — it is possible or permissible / it is
impossible or not permissible.

These expressions are used with infinitives. The person
experiencing the condition may also be added, and will be
in the dative case:

Нельзя шуметь. (It is not permissible to make noise [here].)
Детям можно играть в саду. (The children can play in the yard [it is permitted].)

Не надо can also be used when something is not advised or allowed, but it is milder than нельзя. It is usually translated as "don't" or "[you] shouldn't":

Не надо это делать. (Don't do that.)

To form the past or the future tense in modal expressions, place было (for past) or будет (for future) immediately after the modal term:

Мне надо будет поехать в город. (I will need to go to the city.)
Детям нельзя было выйти на улицу. (The children couldn't go outside.)

Since there is no subject in the nominative with надо / нужно / необходимо and можно / нельзя, было and будет do not change their form, because they have nothing with which to agree.

These sentences may seem a bit odd—the future tense of быть together with an imperfective infinitive is a familiar combination, but other combinations of быть and infinitives are not. These constructions are not some unusual kind of compound verb forms, however. Although they stand next to each other in the sentences, the various forms of быть and the infinitives do not really go together. They each have their own separate function. Быть is necessary in order to indicate whether the necessity, possibility, or impossibility lies in the past or future. The infinitive indicates what action was necessary, possible, or impossible.

Keep in mind that the word order in these modal constructions is generally: modal term + form of быть + infinitive. Any other kind of word order is rare.

Приходиться and прийтись form the past and future tenses differently, of course, since they are verbs. They follow the pattern of the verb pair ходить / идти (to walk).

Нравиться is generally translated as "to like," while любить is translated as "to love." Although they are sometimes used interchangeably, it is important to keep their differences in mind. Нравиться is used in reference to the impression that one has upon encountering someone or something; любить indicates an enduring emotion toward a person or thing. In general, the first verb implies a milder emotion than the second, whether you are talking about your affection for another person, the game of baseball, or vanilla ice cream.

The dative case must be used with нра́виться to indicate the person experiencing the emotion. The receiver of the affection is in the nominative:

Мне нра́вятся э́ти стихи́. (I like these poems.)

With люби́ть, the person experiencing the emotion is in the nominative, while the receiver of the affection is in the accusative:

Оле́г лю́бит Ма́шу. (Oleg loves Masha.)

§9.3-6 INSTRUMENTAL CASE

The instrumental case endings for nouns are:

	Masculine and Neuter	**Feminine** -а/-я	**Feminine** -ь
Sing.	-ом / -ем / -ём	-ой / -ей / -ёй	-ью
Plur.	-ами / -ями		

-Ом/-ем/-ём is really one ending, -ом, with a soft variant, -ем, and a soft stressed variant, -ём. The same is true for the -а/-я feminine endings. The -ями plural ending is also just a soft variant of the -ами ending. Use the hard variants for hard-stem nouns and the soft variants for soft-stem nouns. Use the soft stressed variants for soft-stem nouns that are stressed on the ending.

Remember that, as always, the spelling rules apply. In particular, watch out for nouns with the *stem* (not the word) ending in ж, ч, ш, щ, or ц. If the stress falls on the ending, use -ом for masculine and neuter and -ой for feminine. If the stress falls elsewhere, use -ем for masculine and neuter and -ей for feminine. These rules apply regardless of the vowel ending, if there is one:

каранда́ш — карандашо́м	pencil
ме́сяц — ме́сяцем	month
лицо́ — лицо́м	face
со́лнце — со́лнцем	sun
свеча́ — свечо́й	candle
учи́тельница — учи́тельницей	teacher (*f.*)

Exceptions

Words ending in -анин/-янин and -онок/-ёнок take the standard instrumental endings, but, as always, the stem is changed in the plural:

англича́нином — англича́нами	Englishman/English people
котёнком — котя́тами	kitten/s

Note the fleeting vowel in the instrumental singular of котёнок. The vowel will fall out in the instrumental singular of all words ending in -онок/-ёнок.

The words брат, друг, муж, сын, стул, and лист are not irregular, but they have a stem change in their plural form. They take the soft ending in the instrumental plural:

бра́том — бра́тьями	brother/s
дру́гом — друзья́ми	friend/s
му́жем — мужья́ми	husband/s
сы́ном — сыновья́ми	son/s
сту́лом — сту́льями	chair/s
листо́м — ли́стьями	leaf/leaves

Note the consonant mutation in друзья́ми and the expanded stem in сыновья́ми.

The nouns сосе́д and чёрт (neighbor; devil) are soft in the plural and therefore take the soft variant in the instrumental plural.

In the neuter, the irregular -мя nouns take -ем in the instrumental singular (и́менем) (name) and a hard ending in the instrumental plural (имена́ми).

Де́рево (tree) has the same instrumental plural ending as masculine words like брат: дере́вьями.

In the feminine, the noun мать (mother) takes the expected instrumental endings, but дочь (daughter) has an irregular instrumental plural ending, -ьми (-ями, however, is also possible). Remember to use the expanded stem in both the singular and the plural: ма́терью — матеря́ми / до́черью — дочерьми́.

The feminine noun це́рковь (church), which is ordinarily soft, takes a hard ending in the instrumental plural: церква́ми. In addition, it does not lose the fleeting vowel in the instrumental singular: це́рковью. The same is true for любо́вь (love) (see appendix).

The feminine nouns ло́шадь and дверь (horse; door) can take either the standard instrumental plural ending for soft stems or the irregular ending also used for дочь (see above). For ло́шадь, the irregular ending is more likely: лошадьми́. For дверь, the standard ending is more common: дверя́ми.

Two words that exist only in the plural also take the irregular instrumental plural ending. Unlike ло́шадь and дверь, they **always** take the irregular ending: детьми́, людьми́ (children; people).

The instrumental case answers the questions кем? чем? как? (by whom? with what? how?) It has the following functions:

1. It indicates the **"instrument"** with which something is done:

Он пи́шет письмо́ **карандашо́м**. (He's writing the letter with a pencil.)

2. It can also be used in a similar, but more abstract, way to describe the **means** by which something is done:

Они́ прие́хали **по́ездом**. (They arrived by train.)

3. It is used to describe the **manner** in which something is done:

Она́ всегда́ говори́т гро́мким **го́лосом**. (She always speaks in a loud voice.) [See §10 for adjectival endings.]

In this connection, the instrumental can also provide a comparison between two things:

Маши́на промча́лась **стрело́й**. (The car flew by like an arrow. [= Маши́на промча́лась как стрела́.])

4. It denotes the **agent** (that is, the person[s] or thing[s] performing the action of the sentence) **in a passive construction**:

Зада́ча реша́ется **студе́нтами**. (The problem is being solved by the students.)

Adjectives That Take the Instrumental Case

дово́льный (-ое, -ая, -ые) (satisfied)
    short forms—дово́лен, дово́льно, дово́льна, дово́льны
    (and its negation, недово́льный)
бе́дный (-ое, -ая, -ые)   (poor)
    short forms—бе́ден, бе́дно, бедна́, бе́дны
бога́тый (-ое, -ая, -ые)   (rich)
    short forms—бога́т, бога́то, бога́та, бога́ты

Эта страна́ бога́та **не́фтью**. (This country is rich in oil.)
Дово́льный **рабо́той**, он мно́го де́лает. (Happy with his work, he works hard.)

Verbs That Take the Instrumental Case (Verbs of Being and Condition)

The most commonly used are:

(по)каза́ться	to seem
станови́ться / стать	to become
явля́ться / яви́ться	to appear, to be
ока́зываться / оказа́ться	to turn out to be
остава́ться / оста́ться	to stay, to remain

считáться   to be considered

Онá стáла **дóктором**. (She became a doctor.)
Он считáется **хорóшим человéком**. (He is considered a fine person.)
[See §10 for adjectival endings.]

Verbs That Take the Instrumental Case

When used in the following meanings, some commonly used verbs take the instrumental case:

рабóтать	to work (in a trade or profession that is specified)
служи́ть	to serve (in a trade or profession that is specified)
занимáться	to study or be occupied (with something)
(за)интересовáться	to be interested (in something)
увлекáться / увлéчься	to be fascinated or absorbed (by something)
(по)любовáться	to admire (someone or something)
горди́ться	to be proud (of something)
(вос)пóльзоваться	to make use (of something); to profit or benefit (from something)
завéдовать	to manage (some kind of business or professional enterprise)
руководи́ть	to direct (someone or something)
управля́ть	to govern (something)
рисковáть	to risk (something)
(за)болéть	to be ill (with something)

Он рабóтает **инженéром**. (He works as an engineer.)
Роди́тели любýются **ребёнком**. (The parents are admiring their child.)
Мы занимáемся **матемáтикой**. (We're studying mathematics.)

The Verb "To Be" and the Instrumental Case

The verb "to be" can take either the nominative or the instrumental.

1. In the present tense, use the nominative:

Он профéссор. (He's a professor.)

2. In the past and future tenses and with an infinitive, use the instrumental:

Он был профéссором. Он бýдет профéссором. Он хóчет быть профéссором. (He was a professor. He will be a professor. He wants to be a professor.)

It is also possible, in the past and future, but not with the infinitive, to use the nominative: Он был профéссор. But the nominative is much less frequent in such sentences, because its use implies that you have defined the very essence of the individual you are describing.

Prepositions That Take the Instrumental Case

When used in the following meanings, these prepositions take the instrumental:

над	above, over
под	under
пе́ред	in front of; before
за	behind; beyond; for (in the sense of going to fetch something)
ме́жду	between

Ла́мпа виси́т над столо́м. (The lamp is hanging over the table.)
Мяч лежи́т под столо́м. (The ball is lying under the table.)
Де́ти игра́ют пе́ред до́мом. (The children are playing in front of the house.)
Де́ти игра́ют за до́мом. (The children are playing behind the house.)
Он пошёл в магази́н за молоко́м (He went to the store for milk.)
Рабо́чие стро́ят шко́лу ме́жду па́рком и магази́ном. (The workers are building a school between the park and the store.)

The prepositions за and под can also take the accusative (see §9.3-2).

One other preposition takes the instrumental. It may present a bit of a problem.

с   with (in the sense of "together with")

Де́ти пошли́ в кино́ с ма́терью. (The children went to the movies with their mother.)
Я съе́ла хлеб с ма́слом. (I ate some bread with butter.)

You may well think, "why is this preposition necessary, if the instrumental case alone does the same thing?"

Он пи́шет письмо́ карандашо́м. (He is writing the letter *with* a pencil.)

The answer is that sometimes the preposition is needed, and sometimes it is not. When "with" indicates the instrument, means by which, or manner in which something is done, the preposition is omitted and the instrumental alone is sufficient. When "with" refers to that which accompanies something or someone, the preposition is obligatory. Compare these two sentences:

Она́ говори́т гро́мким го́лосом. (She is speaking in a loud voice.)
Она́ говори́т со ста́рым профе́ссором. (She is speaking with the elderly professor.)

Instrumental constructions with с can also be used with abstract nouns:

Она́ говори́т с интере́сом. (She is speaking with interest.)

The preposition с can also take the genitive (see §9.3-3).

§10. Adjectives

§10.1
WHAT ARE
ADJECTIVES?

Adjectives describe or modify nouns or pronouns.

§10.2
FORMATION

In English, adjectives do not change their form. That is not true in Russian: adjectives change their endings to indicate gender, number, and case. The endings used for adjectives differ from those for nouns, so another set of endings must be learned. Fortunately, there are some similarities that make memorization easier.

Different kinds of endings are used for the different types of adjectives. They are all listed and explained in §10.5.

§10.3
AGREEMENT

Generally, adjectives agree in gender, number, and case with the nouns they modify. If a word is, for example, a feminine singular noun in the dative case, then the adjective that modifies it will take the feminine singular dative ending for adjectives.

§10.4
POSITION

Adjectives can directly precede the nouns they modify (that is, they can be in the attributive position), or they can be connected to the noun via the verb (that is, they can be in the predicative position). Some types of adjectives can take only one of these positions, while others can take both. The possible positions for each type of adjective are mentioned in §10.5. For a more detailed explanation of the attributive and predicative positions, see the section "How to Use Short Adjectives" in §10.5-1.

§10.5
TYPES

§10.5-1
DESCRIPTIVE
ADJECTIVES

Long-Form Adjectives

The endings for long-form adjectives are:

	Singular Masculine	Singular Neuter	Singular Feminine	Plural
Nom.	-ый / -ий / -ой	-ое / -ее	-ая / -яя	-ые / -ие
Acc.	like nom. or gen.	-ое / -ее	-ую / -юю	like nom. or gen.

	Singular Masculine	Singular Neuter	Singular Feminine	Plural
Gen.	-ого / -его		-ой / -ей	-ых / -их
Prep.	-ом / -ем		-ой / -ей	-ых / -их
Dat.	-ому / -ему		-ой / -ей	-ым / -им
Inst.	-ым / -им		-ой / -ей	-ыми / -ими

Long-form adjectives agree in gender, number, and case with the nouns they modify. (The uses of each case will not be discussed here: they were covered in the section on nouns, §9.) Long-form adjectives generally precede the nouns they modify (that is, they are in the attributive position), but can take the predicative position as well.

Although the chart above lists pairs of endings, the pairs really represent one ending: for example, -ая is the hard variant for feminine nominative singular and -яя is the soft variant. Use the hard variants for hard-stem adjectives and soft variants for soft-stem adjectives. Remember that, as always, the spelling rules apply.

There is an additional third ending for masculine nominative and accusative singular: -ой. It is used for those masculine adjectives which take the stress on the ending: молодой (young). In all other cases, such adjectives will take the regular hard adjective endings. Neuter and feminine adjectives with stress on the ending do not have special endings and are treated like any other adjectives.

The masculine and plural forms in the accusative can be like either the nominative or the genitive forms. Use the nominative forms when the noun that the adjective is modifying is inanimate; use the genitive forms when the noun that the adjective is modifying is animate. As stated in §9.3-2, inanimate nouns refer to things or concepts, and animate nouns refer to people or animals. Words that designate groups of people, however, are treated as inanimate:

народ (nation, people)
отряд (military detachment)
класс (class)

Short-Form Adjectives

Some adjectives have short forms in addition to the long forms described above. (Adjectives that end in -ский and many adjectives that end in -ний have no short forms.)

The endings for short-form adjectives are:

	Singular Masculine	Singular Neuter	Singular Feminine	Plural
Nom.	-	-o	-a	-ы / -и

Short-form adjectives agree in gender and number with the nouns they modify. Note that the short forms exist only in the nominative. Use the hard plural variant for hard-stem nouns in the plural and the soft plural variant for soft-stem nouns in the plural. Be sure to apply the spelling rules.

If the stem ends in a consonant cluster, an inserted vowel may be needed between the last two consonants in the masculine short form. When the cluster consists of a hard consonant + к, the inserted vowel will be -o-: сла́дкий — сла́док (sweet).

The vowel -o- is also needed for по́лон (full), смешо́н (funny), and до́лог (long).

When the cluster consists of a soft consonant + к, the inserted vowel will be -e-: го́рький — го́рек (bitter).

The vowel -e- is also used if the cluster consists of a consonant + н: больно́й — бо́лен (sick), у́мный — умён (smart), споко́йный — споко́ен (calm).

Note that neither the soft sign nor -й- remains once the vowel is inserted. The vowel -e- is also needed for све́тел (light—in reference to brightness) and хитёр (sly).

A vowel is never inserted between с and т: пусто́й — пуст (empty).

The adjectives большо́й (big) and ма́ленький (small) have special short forms:

большо́й — вели́к (-о́, -а́, -и́)
ма́ленький — мал (-о́, -а́, -ы́)

Some adjectives that end in -нный or -нний in the long form take -ен in the short form, and others take -енен:

уве́ренный — уве́рен	certain, convinced
ограни́ченный — ограни́чен	limited
и́скренний — и́скренен	sincere
обыкнове́нный — обыкнове́нен	ordinary

If the stem of a short-form adjective has three or more syllables, its stress is the same as that of the long form. For most shorter adjectives, it is also the same, but in some adjectives the stress shifts to the ending for the feminine (бы́стро — быстра́) (fast).

How to Use Short Adjectives

As you know, long-form adjectives usually precede the noun they modify:

Краси́вое де́рево (a beautiful tree [attributive position])

They can also follow the noun:

Де́рево краси́вое (the tree is beautiful [predicative position])

The difference in these two examples is not simply a matter of word order—these are actually very different constructions. This becomes clear when they are put into full sentences that contain verbs:

Краси́вое де́рево растёт о́коло реки́. (A beautiful tree is growing by the river.)
Э́то де́рево бы́ло о́чень краси́вое. (That tree was very beautiful.)

In the second example, the adjective modifies the noun not directly but through the verb (hence it is said to be in the predicative position). In some cases, the verb may be understood but not expressed:

Де́рево краси́вое. (The tree is beautiful.)

Nevertheless, such sentences are complete.

While long-form adjectives can be used either in the attributive or the predicative position, short-form adjectives can be used only in the predicative position. The link verb быть is used in the past and future, and is understood in the present tense.

Sometimes the use of the short form instead of the long form in a sentence changes the meaning slightly. The long form can imply a long-standing condition. For example, Он бо́лен means that he is sick now, while Он больно́й indicates that he suffers from a recurring or chronic illness.

In addition, the short form is used when reference is being made to a specific rather than a general situation:

Э́тот челове́к стар для неё. (That man is [too] old for her.)

In other words, that man may not be old in absolute terms, but he is old relative to her.

The short form is also used when всё, э́то, or что (all, that, what) is in the subject position.

Я чита́ю то, что интере́сно. (I read that which is interesting.)
Э́то пло́хо. (That's bad.)

Дóлжен, должнá, должнó, должны́ and нýжен, нужнá, нýжно, нýжны

Two particularly important short adjectival forms need to be mentioned here as well. The modal adjectives дóлжен, должнá, должнó, должны́ (ought, should) serve a function similar to that of нáдо / нýжно / необходи́мо (see §9.3-5), but in sentences with дóлжен, должнá, должнó, должны́, the person experiencing the condition is in the nominative case, not the dative. As a result, there must be agreement in gender and number:

Марк дóлжен занимáться. (Mark ought to study.)

There is little difference in meaning between дóлжен constructions and нáдо / нýжно constructions, but when there is a subject in the nominative, it is more "responsible" for the action of the sentence. When the person is in the dative, on the other hand, he or she is more a "receiver" than an initiator.

The short adjectives нýжен, нужнá, нýжно, нýжны (to be needed) are not to be confused with the invariable modal term нýжно mentioned in §9.3-5. They are used with nouns rather than infinitives:

Мне нужнá кни́га. [I need a book.]
(Compare: Мне нýжно читáть. [I need to read.])

Notice that the person or thing that is needed is in the nominative and that the person needing it is in the dative. There must be agreement in gender and number between the word that is in the nominative and the form of нýжно in these constructions.

To form the past or the future tense in a дóлжен or нýжен construction, place the appropriate form of быть immediately after the term. There must be agreement: in the past tense, быть must agree in number and gender with the subject; in the future, it must agree in number and person.

Он дóлжен был вернýть э́ту кни́гу. (He should have returned that book.)
Мы должны́ бýдем приéхать рáньше. (We will have to arrive earlier.)

These sentences may seem a bit odd—the future tense of быть together with an imperfective infinitive is a familiar combination, but other combinations of быть and infinitives are not. These constructions are not some unusual kind of compound verb forms, however. Although they stand next to each other in the sentences, the various forms of быть and the infinitives do not really go together. They each have their own separate function. Быть is necessary in order to indicate whether the necessity lies in the past or future. The infinitive indicates what action was necessary.

Keep in mind that the word order in these constructions is generally: form of должен or нужен + form of быть + infinitive. Any other kind of word order is rare.

§10.5-2 POSSESSIVE ADJECTIVES AND PRONOUNS

In Russian, the forms for possessive adjectives are identical to those for possessive pronouns. You use the same forms, whether you are modifying a noun or replacing it.

Possessive adjectives and pronouns are used to indicate who "possesses" the nouns they modify or replace:

Наши дети уже ходят в школу. (Our children already attend school.)
—Чья это тетрадь? —Эта тетрадь моя. ("Whose notebook is that?" "That notebook is mine.")

The forms for possessive adjectives and pronouns are:

	Singular Masculine	Singular Neuter	Singular Feminine	Plural
Nom.	мой/наш	моё/наше	моя/наша	мои/наши
Acc.	like nom. or gen.	моё/наше	мою/нашу	like nom. or gen.
Gen.	моего / нашего		моей/нашей	моих/ наших
Prep.	моём / нашем		моей/нашей	моих/ наших
Dat.	моему / нашему		моей/нашей	моим/ нашим
Inst.	моим / нашим		моей/нашей	моими/ нашими

Твой (your [singular]) and свой (one's own) are declined in the same way as мой (my). Ваш (your [plural and formal]) is declined in the same way as наш (our).

All the possessive adjectives and pronouns above agree in gender, number, and case with the nouns to which they refer. The adjectives can be used attributively or predicatively.

The masculine and plural forms in the accusative can be either like the nominative or like the genitive forms. Use the nominative forms when the noun to which the adjective or pronoun refers is inanimate. Use the genitive forms when the noun is animate. See §9.3-2 or §10.5-1 for a definition of animate and inanimate.

Something is missing from the above charts, of course—the third-person forms. (First-person forms refer to I and we, second-person forms to you [singular and plural], and third-person forms to he, she, it, and they.) They were left out because they are rather unusual. They do not change their form but are always:

егó	his, its
её	her
их	their

They have the same form as the third-person singular and plural personal pronouns in the accusative and genitive, but the context will make it possible to distinguish between them.

One other potential source of ambiguity needs to be discussed here—if you say "he took his book," do you mean that he took his own book or someone else's? In English, the problem is resolved by adding words like "own" or by relying on the context to make it clear. In Russian, another possessive form must be used: свой (one's own [mentioned above]).

Only свой can be used when you are referring to the subject of the sentence or clause:

Сáша взял свою кнѝгу. (Sasha took his own book.)

As a result, when you say, "Сáша взял егó кнѝгу" (Sasha took his book), it is clear that you are referring to someone else's book, not Sasha's book.

Note that because свой is used to refer to the subject, it cannot be attached as a modifier to the subject itself.

As mentioned in §9.3-5, some sentences do not have a subject in the nominative; the person who performs the action of the sentence is in the dative case. In such sentences, свой is still used:

Емý нáдо взять свою кнѝгу. (He needs to take his own book.)

While свой is obligatory in the third person in order to avoid ambiguity, it is optional in the first and second persons. Both of the following variants are acceptable and interchangeable:

Я взялá мою кнѝгу. / Я взялá свою кнѝгу. (I took my book.)
Ты взял твою кнѝгу. / Ты взял свою кнѝгу. (You took your book.)

§10.5-3 DEMON-STRATIVE ADJECTIVES AND PRONOUNS

In Russian, the forms for demonstrative adjectives are identical to those for demonstrative pronouns. You use the same forms, whether you are modifying a noun or replacing it.

Demonstrative adjectives and pronouns are used to "point out" the nouns they modify or replace:

Пу́шкин жил в э́том до́ме. (Pushkin lived in this house.)
—Каки́е кни́ги возьмёт Гри́ша? —Он возьмёт э́ти.
   ("Which books will Grisha take?" "He'll take these.")

The forms for demonstrative adjectives and pronouns are:

	Singular Masculine	Singular Neuter	Singular Feminine	Plural
Nom.	э́тот / тот	э́то / то	э́та / та	э́ти / те
Acc.	like nom. or gen.	э́то / то	э́ту / ту	like nom. or gen.
Gen.	э́того / того́		э́той / той	э́тих / тех
Prep.	э́том / том		э́той / той	э́тих / тех
Dat.	э́тому / тому́		э́той / той	э́тим / тем
Inst.	э́тим / тем		э́той / той	э́тими / те́ми

All the demonstrative adjectives and pronouns above agree in gender, number, and case with the nouns to which they refer. The adjectives are used attributively.

The masculine and plural forms in the accusative can be either like the nominative or like the genitive forms. Use the nominative forms when the noun to which the adjective or pronoun refers is inanimate. Use the genitive forms when the noun is animate. See §9.3-2 or §10.5-1 for a definition of animate and inanimate.

Э́тот (this, that) is used more frequently than тот (that). Тот is used most often in combination with э́тот to express a contrast:

Э́тот студе́нт пришёл на ле́кцию, а тот студе́нт пое́хал на пляж.
   (This student came to the lecture, and that student went to the beach.)

When a contrast is not expressed in a sentence, э́тот can be translated as "that."

Тот has an additional function, in complex sentences, which will be discussed in §11.4.

§10.5-4 INTERROGATIVE ADJECTIVES

Interrogative adjectives ask a question about the nouns they modify:

Чья маши́на стои́т на у́лице? (Whose car is standing on the street?)

The forms of чей (whose) listed below are also used when чей is an interrogative pronoun (see §11.3). But the interrogative adjective modifies nouns, while the interrogative pronoun replaces nouns.

The forms for interrogative adjectives are:

	Singular Masculine	Singular Neuter	Singular Feminine	Plural
Nom.	чей	чьё	чья	чьи
Acc.	like nom. or gen.	чьё	чью	like nom. or gen.
Gen.	чьего́		чьей	чьих
Prep.	чьём		чьей	чьих
Dat.	чьему́		чьей	чьим
Inst.	чьим		чьей	чьи́ми

(Two other interrogative adjectives, како́й and кото́рый [both mean what, which], take standard adjectival endings and their forms will therefore not be listed here.)

There is, of course, agreement in gender, number, and case with the noun. These adjectives are generally used attributively. For чей, the masculine and plural forms in the accusative can be either like the nominative or like the genitive forms. Use the nominative forms when the noun is inanimate, and the genitive forms when it is animate. See §9.3-2 or §10.5-1 for a definition of animate and inanimate.

§10.5-5 COMPARATIVE ADJECTIVES

There are two kinds of comparative adjectives. Simple comparatives are invariable and are generally used predicatively. Compound comparatives agree in gender, number, and case with the nouns they modify and are generally used attributively.

To create a compound comparative, place the adverb бо́лее **(more)** or ме́нее **(less)** in front of a descriptive adjective:

бо́лее интере́сный фильм (a more interesting film)

The formation of the simple comparative, on the other hand, requires new endings. The ending -ee (or, less commonly, -ей) is added to the adjectival stem:

э́тот фильм интере́снее (this film is more interesting)

The ending -e is added to adjectival stems ending in к, г, х, д, т, or ст. Consonant mutation occurs in such words:

гро́мкий — гро́мче (loud/louder)
чи́стый — чи́ще (clean/cleaner)

Some adjectival stems that end in -к or -ок drop the -к or -ок **and** have mutation of the consonant that precedes it:

бли́зкий — бли́же (close/closer)

See the appendix for a chart on consonant mutation.

In comparatives that end in -ee, the stress usually falls on the first -e of the ending. If there are three or more syllables, the stress is the same as for the long-form adjective. Comparatives that end in -e are never stressed on the ending. The stress falls on the second-to-last syllable.

EXCEPTIONS

The Compound Comparative

Several adjectives, in addition to the standard compound comparative forms, have irregular forms as well:

ма́ленький — ме́ньший	small/smaller
большо́й — бо́льший	big/bigger
плохо́й — ху́дший	bad/worse
хоро́ший — лу́чший	good/better
высо́кий — вы́сший	high/higher (in an abstract sense)
ни́зкий — ни́зший	low/lower (in an abstract sense)
молодо́й — мла́дший	young/younger, junior
ста́рый — ста́рший	old/older, senior

Note that there is little difference in spelling between большо́й and бо́льший. In cases other than the nominative, only the stress distinguishes the two forms. When the last two words in the list, молодо́й and ста́рый, take the standard compound comparative form, the meaning is strictly chronological:

бо́лее молодо́й (younger in age)
бо́лее ста́рый (older in age)

The Simple Comparative

Some adjectives have irregular simple comparative forms:

ма́ленький — ме́ньше	small/smaller
большо́й — бо́льше	big/bigger
плохо́й — ху́же	bad/worse
хоро́ший — лу́чше	good/better
ста́рый — ста́рше	old/older (used for people)
— старе́е	old/older (used for things)
то́нкий — то́ньше	thin/thinner
до́лгий — до́льше	long/longer (used for time or distance)
далёкий — да́льше	far/farther
глубо́кий — глу́бже	deep/deeper
дешёвый — деше́вле	cheap/cheaper

Additional Points

Some adjectives have no comparative forms because their meaning makes it impossible to use them comparatively: деревя́нный дом (a wooden house).

Adjectives that end in -ский or -овый lack simple comparative forms, but do possess compound comparative forms. In addition, the following adjectives have only compound comparative forms:

ра́нний	early
ли́шний	superfluous
го́рдый	proud
уста́лый	tired
пло́ский	flat

The prefix по- is sometimes added to simple comparative forms to give the meaning "somewhat":

Он помоло́же. (He's somewhat younger.)

The Use of Чем

In order to state a comparison between two things, use the word чем (than):

У него́ бо́лее краси́вый автомоби́ль, чем у меня́. (He has a more beautiful car than I do.)

When using the simple comparative and comparing declinable nouns in the nominative case, you may omit чем:

Па́вел ста́рше, чем Са́ша.   Pavel is older than Sasha.
Па́вел ста́рше Са́ши.   Pavel is older than Sasha.

Remember to put the second noun into the genitive after omitting чем.

If you want to quantify the difference between the two things you are comparing, use на ско́лько (by how much) in the question and на (by) in the answer:

На ско́лько Па́вел ста́рше Са́ши? Па́вел на де́сять лет ста́рше Са́ши.
(By how much is Pavel older than Sasha? Pavel is older than Sasha by ten years.)

§10.5-6 SUPERLATIVE ADJECTIVES

There are two kinds of superlative adjectives, simple superlatives and compound superlatives. Both kinds agree in gender, number, and case with the nouns they modify, and both can be used either predicatively or attributively.

Oddly enough, even though it is called a superlative, the simple superlative expresses the existence of a high degree of a quality, but not the highest degree (он умне́йший ма́льчик — he's a very smart boy). The object of comparison, in fact, is often absent from the sentence. The compound superlative, on the other hand, does express the **highest** degree of a quality. The compound superlative is used much more often than the simple superlative.

To create a compound superlative, place the adjective са́мый (most), with an agreeing adjectival ending on it, in front of a descriptive adjective:

са́мая краси́вая карти́на (the most beautiful painting)

The formation of the simple superlative is more complicated, because it requires new endings. The suffix -ейш- is added to the adjectival stem, and long adjectival endings are added to the suffix (in accordance with the spelling rules):

краси́вейшая карти́на (a very beautiful painting)

The suffix -айш- is added to adjectival stems ending in к, г, х, ж, ч, ш, or щ. Consonant mutation occurs in such words; for example:

вели́кий — велича́йший (great/very great)

See the appendix for a chart on consonant mutation.

The same rules for stress apply as for simple comparatives ending in -ее.

EXCEPTIONS

The Compound Superlative

Several adjectives do not take the standard compound superlative forms, but irregular forms instead. They are the same adjectives that have irregular forms in the compound comparative. Because the forms they take in the compound superlative are identical to the ones they take in the compound comparative, they will not be listed again here. See

§10.5-5. Because the forms are identical, and because ambiguity may result, all these compound superlatives are sometimes used with са́мый: Э́то са́мый лу́чший подхо́д. (That's the best approach.)

The Simple Superlative

There is an irregular simple superlative for ма́ленький (ма́лый): мале́йший (smallest). It usually occurs in set expressions:

> Он не име́ет ни мале́йшего поня́тия. (He doesn't have the slightest idea.)

In other situations, use the compound superlative са́мый ма́ленький. In addition, use the compound superlative form instead of a simple superlative form for the other adjectives that are listed as irregular in the simple comparative:

большо́й — са́мый большо́й	big/biggest
плохо́й — са́мый плохо́й	bad/worst
хоро́ший — са́мый хоро́ший	good/best
ста́рый — са́мый ста́рый	old/oldest
то́нкий — са́мый то́нкий	thin/thinnest
до́лгий — са́мый до́лгий	long/longest (used for time or distance)
далёкий — са́мый далёкий	far/farthest
глубо́кий — са́мый глубо́кий	deep/deepest
дешёвый — са́мый дешёвый	cheap/cheapest

A number of other adjectives lack a simple superlative form. Among them are:

> ра́нний (early)
> молодо́й (young)
> родно́й (own, native)
> больно́й (sick)
> делово́й (businesslike)

The Use of Всего́ and Всех

The superlative can also be formed by using a **comparative** adjective together with всего́ (all, everything) for things or всех (all, everybody) for people, but only in a predicative position:

> Она́ занима́ется бо́льше всех. (She studies more than everybody [else].)

Such a construction stresses the superlative nature of the quality described.

§10.5-7 SUBSTAN- TIVIZED ADJECTIVES

A substantivized adjective is an adjective that has become a "substance," that is, it represents a thing, not a quality. How does that happen? A term (for example, бу́лочная ла́вка [bakery]) is used frequently and, after a while, a kind of shorthand develops in common usage—the noun is omitted in conversation, but it is still understood to be present. The adjective alone comes to stand for the entire term. It is essentially a noun from the semantic point of view, but from the grammatical point of view, it is an adjective.

The substantivized adjective keeps the gender of the noun that was originally present. It keeps its adjectival endings and is always declined like an adjective. When necessary, it can be used like a regular adjective, that is, with a noun that is present. But it is most frequently used as a substantivized adjective.

Some common substantivized adjectives are:

столо́вая (ко́мната)	dining room
гости́ная (ко́мната)	living room
шампа́нское (вино́)	champagne
учёный (челове́к)	scholar, scientist
больно́й (челове́к)	sick person
взро́слый (челове́к)	adult
рабо́чие (лю́ди)	workers
бу́дущее (вре́мя)	the future

§11.

Pronouns

Pronouns replace nouns that have already been mentioned in the sentence or in a previous sentence.

Personal pronouns replace nouns that refer to people or things: Ко́ля был в магази́не. Сейча́с **он** до́ма. (Kolya was at the store. Now **he's** home.) They are divided into singular and plural and into first, second, and third person:

	Singular	Plural
First Person	я (I)	мы (we)
Second Person	ты (you)	вы (you)
Third Person	он, оно́, она́ (he, it, she)	они́ (they)

The forms for personal pronouns are:

Singular					
			Masculine	**Neuter**	**Feminine**
Nom.	я	ты	он	оно́	она́
Acc.	меня́	тебя́	его́		её
Gen.	меня́	тебя́	его́		её
Prep.	мне	тебе́	нём		ней
Dat.	мне	тебе́	ему́		ей
Inst.	мной	тобо́й	им		ей (е́ю)

84

Plural			
Nom.	мы	вы	они́
Acc.	нас	вас	их
Gen.	нас	вас	их
Prep.	нас	вас	них
Dat.	нам	вам	им
Inst.	на́ми	ва́ми	и́ми

The feminine instrumental singular е́ю is sometimes used when there is a possibility of confusion with the feminine dative singular. Generally, however, the ей form is used.

All the personal pronouns above agree in number, case, and person with the nouns they replace. In the third person singular, they also agree in gender.

The prepositions к, в, с, под, над, and пе́ред generally require -о on the end when they precede мне or мной:

Он до́лго говори́л со мной. (He talked with me for a long time.)

The preposition о takes the form обо when it occurs in front of мне.

Third-person pronouns in cases other than the nominative require an н- at the beginning **if** they are governed by a preposition:

Он занима́ется с ни́ми. (He is studying with them.)

Remember, however, that this rule applies only to pronouns. Do not use н- when using его́, её, and их as possessive adjectives:

Мать говори́ла с ним, but Мать говори́ла с его́ учи́телем. (Mother spoke with him; Mother spoke with his teacher.)
(See §10.5-2 on possessive adjectives.)

Unlike I, я is not capitalized. In addition, keep in mind that вы is used both as the plural form of you and as the formal singular form. It generally takes plural verb forms and plural predicative adjectives even when referring to only one person. (See §8 on the use of ты vs. the use of вы.)

§11.3 INTERRO-GATIVE PRONOUNS

Interrogative pronouns ask a question about the nouns they replace:

—**Кто** поéхал в гóрод? —Дéдушка поéхал в гóрод.
("Who went to the city?" "Grandfather went to the city.")

The same forms of чей (whose) are used for both the interrogative pronoun and the interrogative adjective (see §10.5-4); because the forms are identical, they will not be repeated here. Remember that the interrogative pronoun replaces nouns, while the interrogative adjective modifies them.

In addition to чей, there are several other interrogative pronouns: кто (who) and что (what). Their forms are:

Nom.	кто	что
Acc.	когó	что
Gen.	когó	чегó
Prep.	ком	чём
Dat.	комý	чемý
Inst.	кем	чем

Кто is treated as masculine and singular, even though it does not always refer to masculine and singular nouns:

—Кто здесь был? —Здесь были Лéна и Кóля. ("Who was here?" "Lena and Kolya were here.")

Note the change in the verb in the answer.

Like any noun or pronoun, кто must take the case that is required by the sentence:

—Комý он принёс яблоко? —Учйтелю. ("To whom did he bring the apple?" "To the teacher.")

Что is treated as neuter and singular, even though it does not always refer to neuter and singular nouns:

—Что было в магазйне? —В магазйне были брюки, блýзки, плáтья и пальтó. ("What was in the store?" "There were pants, blouses, dresses, and coats in the store.")

Note the change in the verb in the answer.

Like any noun or pronoun, что must take the case that is required by the sentence:

Чегó нé было в магазйне? (What was not in the store?)

§11.4 RELATIVE PRONOUNS

All interrogative pronouns can be used as relative pronouns. Relative pronouns introduce the subordinate clause of complex sentences. They refer to nouns that were previously mentioned in the main clause (these nouns are called antecedents):

> Мы говори́ли с людьми́, **кото́рые** неда́вно верну́лись из Москвы́. (We were speaking to some people who recently returned from Moscow.)

Кото́рые refers to and stands in for людьми́, the antecedent. The main clause, мы говори́ли с людьми́, can stand on its own as a sentence. The subordinate clause, кото́рые неда́вно верну́лись из Москвы́, cannot exist as a full sentence without the main clause. (Keep in mind that the relative clause must be set off from the main clause by commas.)

The relative pronouns кто, что, чей, and кото́рый also have functions as other types of pronouns or adjectives. Кото́рый, as a relative pronoun, means who, which, or that. The others have the same meanings as they do in their other functions: кто (who), что (what, that), and чей (whose). See §11.3 for the declension of кто and что and §10.5-4 for the declension of чей and кото́рый. Because the declensions are the same, they will not be repeated here.

Кото́рый agrees in gender and number with the noun that it replaces. It does not agree in case; its case is determined by the grammatical function of кото́рый within the subordinate clause.

The antecedent of кто is masculine, singular, and animate. The antecedent of что is neuter, singular, and inanimate. Кто and что do not have nouns as antecedents, only pronouns. The most common are тот for кто and то for что. Тот, кто means "he who" and то, что means "that which." (This is an additional use of the demonstrative pronoun тот. For a discussion of demonstrative pronouns and the declension of тот, see §10.5-3.)

The pronoun все (all) can be used with кто as well. Although it refers to more than one person, it is used as a collective, takes singular verbs, and is treated like a masculine singular pronoun in these types of sentences:

> Это бы́ло интере́сно всем, кто прие́хал на ле́кцию. (That was interesting for everyone who came to the lecture.)

The neuter pronoun всё (all) can be used in a similar way with что:

> Он сде́лал всё, что ну́жно. (He did everything that was necessary.)

Sometimes the antecedent is unstated in sentences with кто or что. Кто may refer to an unstated person, and что may refer to an unstated thing:

Я не зна́ю, кто там был. (I don't know who was there.)

Чей can also be used in this way when there is a reference to an unstated person, and when possession needs to be indicated.

§11.5 REFLEXIVE PRONOUNS

The reflexive pronoun себя refers to (or "reflects") the subject of the sentence or clause:

Серёжа купи́л себе́ автомоби́ль. (Seryozha bought himself a car.)

The forms of the reflexive pronoun are:

Nom.	——
Acc.	себя
Gen.	себя
Prep.	себе́
Dat.	себе́
Inst.	собо́й

Себя does not have a nominative form because it refers to the subject and therefore cannot be the subject itself. It is a fairly easy pronoun to use—it does not change for gender, number, or person. As a result, its exact translation will vary, depending on the subject:

Серёжа купи́л себе́ автомоби́ль. (Seryozha bought *himself* a car.)
Мы купи́ли себе́ автомоби́ль. (We bought *ourselves* a car.)

It can be translated as myself, yourself, himself, itself, herself, ourselves, yourselves, or themselves.

§11.6 INTENSIVE PRONOUNS

Intensive pronouns emphasize or underscore nouns and pronouns:

Он **сам** туда́ пое́хал. (He went there himself.)

They are unusual in that they do not replace anything, but are used **together with** nouns and pronouns. Generally, when intensive pronouns are used with pronouns, they are placed immediately after the pronoun. When used with nouns, they immediately precede the noun.

The forms for intensive pronouns in the nominative case are:

Masculine	Neuter	Feminine	Plural
сам	само́	сама́	са́ми

In the other cases, they take standard **long-form** adjectival endings. In the singular, hard variant endings are used, and in the plural, soft. There are, however, a few exceptions: the masculine and neuter instrumental ending is soft, and the feminine accusative form is саму́.

All forms are stressed on the ending except the nominative plural.

Intensive pronouns agree in gender, number, and case with the words they emphasize.

§11.7 INDEFINITE PRONOUNS

Indefinite pronouns refer to people or objects that are not or cannot be identified:

Кто-то пришёл. (Someone has arrived.)

They are formed by adding -то or -нибу́дь to the interrogative pronouns кто, что, and чей. See §11.3 for a description of interrogative pronouns and for the declension of кто and что. See §10.5-4 for the declension of чей. -То and -нибу́дь do not change for case and are merely added to the various case forms of the interrogative pronouns.

When do you use -то and when do you use -нибу́дь? -То is needed when the person or object in question exists:

Кто-то тебе́ звони́л сего́дня. (Someone called you today.)

In other words, someone called, but the speaker does not know his or her identity. -Нибу́дь is used when the existence of the person or object is uncertain:

Кто-нибу́дь звони́л? (Did anyone call?)

The speaker wants to know whether anyone at all called. There may have been no callers.

Чей-то and чей-нибу́дь are used like adjectives:

На столе́ оста́лась чья-то кни́га. (Someone's book was left on the table.)

§11.8 NEGATIVE PRONOUNS

Negative pronouns are the negation of indefinite pronouns (see §11.7). They refer to unidentified people or objects that do not exist or are not present:

Никто́ не пришёл. (No one came.)

They are formed by adding ни- to the interrogative pronouns кто, что, and чей. In contrast to indefinite pronouns, negative pronouns are formed by putting the particle *before* the interrogative pronoun. There is also no hyphen.

See §11.3 for a description of interrogative pronouns and for the declension of кто and что. See §10.5-4 for the declension of чей. Ни- does not change for case and is merely added to the various case forms of the interrogative pronouns.

When used with prepositions, ни- and the interrogative pronoun are split into two words and the preposition is inserted between them:

Мы ни с кем не говори́ли. (We didn't speak to anyone.)

Although English sentences cannot have double negatives, Russian sentences can contain any number of negatives:

Мы ни с кем ни о чём не говори́ли. (We didn't speak to anyone about anything.)

Note that the verb must be negated by the negative particle не.

Ничей is used like an adjective:

Э́то ничья́ кни́га. (That's no one's book.)

§12.

Verbs

§12.1
WHAT ARE
VERBS?

Verbs are words that describe actions, processes, or states.

§12.2
AGREEMENT

Except in the infinitive form (see §12.6), a verb agrees with the subject of the sentence or clause. In the nonpast tenses (that is, present and future), verbs agree in number and person. In the past tense, they agree in gender and number.

§12.3
MOOD

There are three moods in Russian: indicative, imperative, and conditional.

§12.3-1
INDICATIVE
MOOD

The indicative mood is used most often. It is generally used for statements of fact:

Они живут в деревне. (They live in the country.)
Что ты читаешь? (What are you reading?)

The imperative and the conditional are used in quite limited circumstances, and the indicative applies in all situations where the imperative and the conditional do not (see §12.3-2 for the imperative and §12.3-3 for the conditional).
The indicative is the only mood that reflects tense.

§12.3-2
IMPERATIVE
MOOD

The imperative mood is needed when giving commands or making requests:

Не мешай мне! (Don't bother me!)
Купите, пожалуйста, молока. (Please buy some milk.)

For the formation of the imperative, see §12.8.

§12.3-3
CONDITIONAL
MOOD

The conditional is used to indicate an action that could have occurred (but did not) or may occur under certain (possible or impossible) circumstances:

Если бы у меня были деньги, я бы поступила в университет. (If I had had the money, I would have gone to college.)
Они с удовольствием приехали бы к нам в гости. (They would gladly come to visit us.)

Éсли он вернётся в семь часо́в, мы пойдём в кино́. (If he returns at seven o'clock, we'll go to the movies.)

For the formation of the conditional, see §12.9.

§12.4 ASPECT

Aspect is considered one of the most difficult topics in Russian grammar, but it is less complex than it seems. It may appear daunting because the selection of aspect requires taking a number of points into consideration before making a decision that amounts to a judgment call. Unfortunately, the process is not clear-cut. The selection of aspect does, however, become easier with practice.

It helps to keep in mind that aspect is not an arbitrary and unnecessary complication of Russian grammar. It may appear that way, because English does not have or need aspects. English, however, has many more tenses than does Russian. Because Russian has only three tenses, it would be difficult to express all possible temporal situations without the use of aspect.

The Characteristics of the Aspects

What, exactly, is aspect? There are two aspects, the imperfective and the perfective. Verbs that are imperfective emphasize processes, while verbs that are perfective emphasize results.

Imperfective verb—focus on the process of reading.

Она́ чита́ла кни́гу. (She was reading a book.)

We do not know, on the basis of the sentence above, whether she finished the book. She may or may not have finished it. That is unimportant for the speaker of the above sentence. The speaker concentrates on specifying the activity that was performed.

Perfective verb—focus on the results of reading.

Она́ прочита́ла кни́гу. (She read the book.)

We know, on the basis of the sentence above, that she finished the book. That information is important to the speaker, who conveys it by using the perfective aspect.

Under what circumstances would the process be emphasized, rather than the result?

1. When there is no wish or need to focus on results, as in the first sentence above, or as in: Мы смотре́ли фильм. (We watched a film.)

2. When the action does not produce any real results: Он жил на на́шей у́лице. (He lived on our street.)

Process versus result is not, however, the only factor in the selection of aspect. If an action occurs habitually or repeatedly, the imperfective must be used:

> Мы часто ужинали в этом ресторане. (We often had dinner in this restaurant.)

Do not assume, however, that you must use the perfective if an action occurs only once. You may use either the perfective or imperfective. Follow the guidelines given earlier: if you want to emphasize process, use the imperfective; if you want to focus on results, use the perfective.

Which aspect do you use if more than one verb appears in a sentence? It depends on the actions being described.

1. Simultaneous actions—use the imperfective

> Мы пили чай и смотрели телевизор. (We were drinking tea and watching television.)

2. Consecutive actions—use the perfective

> Даша открыла шкаф и взяла своё пальто. (Dasha opened the closet and took out her coat.)

Sometimes both the perfective and the imperfective will be necessary in the same sentence:

3. When an action occurs while another action is in process—use the imperfective for the action that is in process, the perfective for the action that "breaks in"

> Я читала когда позвонил Володя. (I was reading when Volodya called.)

(The "continuing" action may be interrupted only momentarily, or it may be permanently interrupted.)

4. When several consecutive actions are followed by an action that emphasizes process—use the perfective for the consecutive actions, the imperfective for the action that emphasizes process

> Он помоется, позавтракает и будет работать. (He will wash up, have breakfast, and begin work.)

(This combination of aspects is rather rare and is used only with the future tense.)

As stated above, the perfective puts emphasis on the results of an action; in other words, it focuses attention on the endpoint of the action. It can also be used when speaking of the starting point of an action:

> Оркестр заиграл. (The orchestra began to play.)

Further, the perfective is used when both the starting point and the endpoint need to be emphasized. In such sentences, the action of the verb is translated as going on "for a while":

Мы посидéли в пáрке и ушлй. (We sat in the park for a while and then left.)

(Generally, as in the example above, these verbs require a second verb in the sentence. Otherwise the sentence sounds unfinished.)

Actions described by imperfective verbs, on the other hand, are open-ended. If they do not refer to processes, then they refer to conditions or states:

Он был в Россйи. (He was in Russia.)

Certain key words in a sentence help to determine which aspect should be selected. Expressions such as всегдá (always), чáсто (frequently), рéдко (rarely), кáждый день (every day), and кáждую недéлю (every week) indicate repeated action, and sentences containing these words generally have imperfective verbs. Terms such as дóлго (for a long time), весь день (all day), and всю недéлю (all week) make reference to the duration of an activity (as opposed to its completion) and also occur with imperfective forms. Words that indicate a summing up (всё [all], наконéц [finally]), and expressions of amount (два письмá [two letters], три кнйги [three books]), indicate a focus on results, and sentences that contain these terms generally employ perfective verbs. Words that refer to a change in conditions (вдруг [suddenly]) also require the perfective.

The following chart summarizes the characteristics and uses of the perfective and the imperfective:

Imperfective	Perfective
processes	results
habitual or repeated actions	
simultaneous actions	consecutive actions
open-ended processes, conditions, or states	the starting point of an action, the endpoint of an action, or the starting point and the endpoint of an action
"interrupted" actions (in sentences with more than one verb)	actions that "interrupt" (in sentences with more than one verb)

The Formation of the Aspects

Most Russian verbs are paired (for example, читáть/ прочитáть [to read]) in an aspectual partnership. One verb of the pair is imperfective, the other is perfective. Glossaries usually list the imperfective verb first. Generally, the verbs in a pair have the same meaning (those that do not will be discussed later). Some verbs are unpaired: for example, принадлежáть (to belong). The perfective form of this verb would be useless, given the meaning of принадлежáть and the function of the perfective.

Many perfective verbs are formed by adding a prefix to the imperfective verb. The most commonly used prefixes are:

по-	сидéть/посидéть	to sit
про-	читáть/прочитáть	to read
при-	готóвить/приготóвить	to prepare
с-	петь/спеть	to sing
за-	кричáть/закричáть	to yell
на-	писáть/написáть	to write

In some cases, the addition of the prefix does not change the meaning of the verb. In other cases, it does: for example, писáть—to write; записáть—to make a note.

Generally, however, the prefix за- denotes the beginning of an action:

заигрáть	to begin to play (in reference to musical performances, not games or sports)
заговорúть	to begin to speak
засмеяться	to begin to laugh
закричáть	to begin to shout

The prefix по- also can indicate the beginning of an action:

Пошёл снег. (It started to snow.)

(По- also has a number of other, more widely used meanings [see below].)

With most verbs, however, the beginning of an action must be indicated by using начинáть/начáть (to begin) in a compound construction:

Мы нáчали рабóтать. (We began to work.)

Unlike за- and some other prefixes, по- is a widely used prefix with a number of meanings:

1. With some verbs, it has the meaning of **time limitation**— to do something "for a while":

посидéть	to sit for a while
почитáть	to read for a while
походить	to walk for a while

погуля́ть	to go for a stroll or an outing
побе́гать	to run around for a while
порабо́тать	to work for a while

2. With other verbs, по- indicates a **single, brief action:**

позвони́ть	to call on the phone (single call)
поцелова́ть	to kiss (single kiss)

A number of questions arise.

How can you tell which prefix to add to a particular imperfective verb if you want to create the perfective form? Some verbs take one prefix, others take another. Unfortunately, the choice of the correct prefix does not follow any particular pattern or rule. There is only one thing to do: when a verb is memorized, both the imperfective and the perfective forms should be memorized.

How can you tell which prefixes change the meaning of a verb and which do not? You cannot tell by looking at the prefix or at the verb. Again, there are no general rules. If you add c- to печь (to bake), you will not change its meaning but will only make it perfective. If you add the same prefix to писа́ть (to write), you will get списа́ть (to copy written material by hand). When adding a prefix to a verb, check your dictionary for the meaning of that verb.

Can more than one prefix be used with a given verb? Yes, but not every verb will take every prefix listed above. There are, however, other prefixes with rather specific meanings that can also be used. As a result, one imperfective verb can have quite a number of perfective counterparts:

писа́ть	(to write)	написа́ть	to write
		пописа́ть	to write for a while
		списа́ть	to copy [by hand]
		переписа́ть	to recopy [by hand]
		записа́ть	to make a note
		подписа́ть	to sign
		вписа́ть	to write in
		описа́ть	to describe

Yet another question arises. Suppose you want to say "she described her trip," and wish to use an **imperfective** verb. What do you do? You have only the perfective описа́ть, given above. But perfective verbs can be turned back into imperfective ones in a way that retains the prefixes and the meaning:

описа́ть → опи́с**ыва**ть

The suffix -ыва- (or the soft variant, -ива-) can be used to convert some prefixed perfectives into prefixed imperfectives.

Some verbs, of course, do not change their meaning when a prefix is added to make them perfective. Such verbs do not form imperfectives by means of -ыва-/-ива- (прочита́ть/прочи́тывать [to read] is an exception to this rule).

Vowel alternation (о-а) occurs in some verbs with -ыва-/-ива- suffixes:

перестро́ить/перестра́ивать (to rebuild)

Consonant mutation also occurs in most of these verbs (and does occur as a rule in verbs ending in -ить):

спроси́ть/спра́шивать (to ask)

The stress never falls on -ыва-/-ива- in verbs that have this suffix.

As you can see, verbs do not really form simple aspectual pairs. It would be more correct to say that they form complex chains.

Other types of verbs experience a change in only one letter between perfective and imperfective. These verbs end in -ить in the perfective and -ать/-ять in the imperfective. (Not all verbs that end in this way belong to this category, but all verbs that belong to it do end in this way.)

реша́ть/реши́ть	to solve, decide
конча́ть/ко́нчить	to finish
изуча́ть/изучи́ть	to study, learn
повторя́ть/повтори́ть	to repeat
выполня́ть/вы́полнить	to fulfill
объясня́ть/объясни́ть	to explain
броса́ть/бро́сить	to throw

Because the distinction between the perfective and imperfective is indicated by the presence of the suffixes -и- or а / я-, the addition of a prefix to these verbs does not change the aspect.

Sometimes consonant mutation occurs in verbs of this type:

отвеча́ть/отве́тить	to answer
защища́ть/защити́ть	to defend

Another group of perfective verbs is made imperfective by the addition of the suffix -ва-. (It includes the unprefixed verb дать [to give].)

дава́ть/дать	to give
задава́ть/зада́ть	to assign, to ask [a question]
узнава́ть/узна́ть	to [try to] find out, to recognize
встава́ть/встать	to get up
забыва́ть/забы́ть	to forget
открыва́ть/откры́ть	to open

одевáть/одéть	to dress
добивáться/добиться	to strive, to achieve

All prefixed forms of дать, знать, and стать belong to this group of verbs. Note that prefixes remain when verbs change from perfective to imperfective.

A number of perfective verbs that describe actions of extremely short duration have the suffix -ну- in the perfective:

кричáть/крикнуть	to shout
чихáть/чихнýть	to sneeze
мелькáть/мелькнýть	to flash, gleam

Note the consonant mutation in the first verb.

Not all verbs of this type, however, refer to actions of short duration:

достигáть/достигнуть	to achieve
отдыхáть/отдохнýть	to rest

Note the vowel alternation in the last verb.

There are unprefixed verbs with the suffix -ну- that are imperfective (for example, сóхнуть [to dry]). The presence of that suffix does not guarantee that a verb is perfective—the aspect must be checked in a dictionary. Dictionary entries for every verb will be marked as perfective or imperfective.

Another category of verbs also undergoes a change in the stem when shifting from perfective to imperfective. In these verbs, -а-/-я- changes to -има- and -а- to -ина- when the perfective verbs are turned into imperfectives:

понимáть/понять	to understand
занимáться/заняться	to occupy oneself
начинáть/начáть	to begin

Two verb pairs are spelled exactly the same way in the perfective and imperfective, and they can be distinguished only by stress. In written works, if there is a possibility of confusion between the two forms, the stress will be added, even if other words in the text are not stressed. Fortunately, the stems of these verbs will be different in the imperfective present and perfective future, although they will be identical in other forms.

разрезáть/разрéзать	to cut up
насыпáть/насыпать	to pour in [in reference to nonliquid substances such as sugar or sand]

PAST TENSE

imperfective: я разреза́ла
perfective: я разре́зала

PRESENT TENSE

imperfective: я разреза́ю, ты разреза́ешь, etc.

FUTURE TENSE

imperfective: я бу́ду разреза́ть, ты бу́дешь разреза́ть, etc.
perfective: я разре́жу, ты разре́жешь, etc.

At the other extreme, some verbs have completely different roots in the perfective and imperfective:

брать/взять	to take
класть/положи́ть	to place, put
говори́ть/сказа́ть	to speak, say
иска́ть/найти́	to [try to] find

In the last two pairs, there is a significant difference in the meaning of the imperfective and perfective forms. Говори́ть means to speak either with someone or to someone. Сказа́ть means to say something to someone. The imperfective form can involve two-way conversation, the perfective form is only one-way:

Мы до́лго говори́ли. (We spoke for a long time.)
Он мне сказа́л, что он поэ́т. (He told me that he's a poet.)

Иска́ть means to look for (to try to find) something or someone; найти́ means to find something or someone.

Several verbs not only differ greatly in the form of the two aspects, but also end in -ся in the imperfective:

сади́ться/сесть	to sit down
ложи́ться/лечь	to lie down
станови́ться/стать	to become

Other aspectual pairs are characterized by a number of changes in the stem. Although these pairs of verbs have the same roots, they experience both vowel and consonant changes:

называ́ть/назва́ть	to name, call
посыла́ть/посла́ть	to send
собира́ть/собра́ть	to gather
умира́ть/умере́ть	to die
помога́ть/помо́чь	to help
зажига́ть/заже́чь	to set fire to
предлага́ть/предложи́ть	to suggest
пропада́ть/пропа́сть	to perish, disappear
спаса́ть/спасти́	to save
выраста́ть/вы́расти	to grow

Finally, some anomalies should be noted here. As stated earlier, the по- prefix generally makes verbs perfective. In the verb pair покупа́ть/купи́ть (to buy), however, покупа́ть is imperfective and купи́ть is perfective.

The vast majority of verbs are either perfective or imperfective. Some verbs can be both (a number of verbs with -ова- have this characteristic). Some of the more common ones are:

иссле́довать	to investigate
телеграфи́ровать	to send a telegram

Special Features of Aspect

1. Aspectual Pairs That Don't Pair Up Exactly
As mentioned earlier, the aspectual pair иска́ть/найти́ is not an exact match, because the two verbs do not have the same meaning. A number of other previously mentioned verbs have a similar difference in meaning. For example:

иска́ть/найти́	to try to find/to find
реша́ть/реши́ть	to try to solve/to solve
достига́ть/дости́гнуть	to try to achieve/to achieve
сдава́ть/сдать	to take an exam [to try to pass an exam]/to pass an exam
догова́риваться/договори́ться	to try to come to an agreement/to come to an agreement
опа́здывать/опозда́ть	to be running late/to be late

Студе́нты до́лго реша́ли тру́дную зада́чу, но они́ её не реши́ли. (For a long time, the students tried to solve the difficult problem, but they couldn't solve it.)
Мы опа́здываем на фильм. Нам на́до спеши́ть. (We're running late for the film. We have to hurry.)

In the last example, it may turn out that they get there in time, but they have reason to believe that they may be late.

2. Imperfective Verbs Denoting Actions That Are Done and Then "Undone"
With some verbs, the past tense of the imperfective may indicate that an action was done and then "undone":

Здесь хо́лодно, потому́ что я открыва́ла окно́, что́бы прове́трить ко́мнату. (It's cold in here because I opened the window to air out the room. [The window is now closed and only the coldness of the room provides evidence that it was open.])

The past tense perfective form of these verbs indicates that an action was done and has **not** been "undone":

Я откры́ла окно́, что́бы прове́трить ко́мнату. (I opened the window to air out the room. [The window is now open.])

Some verbs that have this meaning are:

открыва́ть/откры́ть	to open
закрыва́ть/закры́ть	to close

включа́ть/включи́ть	to turn on
выключа́ть/вы́ключить	to turn off
брать/взять	to take
дава́ть/дать	to give
встава́ть/встать	to get up
приходи́ть/прийти́	to arrive

3. The Negation of the Imperfective and the Perfective

The use of a negated imperfective verb in the past tense means that the subject of the sentence did not perform the action and did not intend to perform it. The use of a negated imperfective verb in the future tense means that the subject will not perform the action and does not intend to perform it.

> Студе́нты не писа́ли эти упражне́ния. (The students didn't do these exercises [and didn't plan to do them].)

A past tense negated perfective verb, on the other hand, indicates that the subject of the sentence intended to perform the action but was thwarted in some way. In the future tense, a negated perfective verb indicates that the subject intends to perform the action, but the action cannot be carried out or completed.

> Студе́нты не напи́шут эти упражне́ния. (The students will not finish these exercises. [Something will prevent them: a lack of time, the difficulty of the exercises, insufficient interest.])

4. Aspect in Dialogue

When a questioner is not concerned about the result of an action, but simply wants to know whether an action took place, he or she will use the imperfective. Generally, the answer, whether it is affirmative or negative, will also be in the imperfective.

> —Де́ти гуля́ли в па́рке? ("The children took a walk in the park?")
> —Да, гуля́ли. ("Yes, they did.")

If a question is perfective, then it implies that the questioner has reason to believe that the action may have taken place.

> —Ты написа́л письмо́? ("Did you write [finish] the letter?")
> —Да, написа́л. ("Yes, I did.")

The questioner knows, from something said or done earlier, that there was an intention to write the letter. He or she is asking about results: has the intended action been accomplished? The answer is perfective if: a) the action was accomplished (Да, написа́л) or b) the action was not accomplished (Нет, не написа́л). It is imperfective if the speaker hasn't done anything, hasn't started it at all (Нет, не писа́л)

Aspect and Infinitives

Verbs do not always appear singly: sometimes an auxiliary verb is used together with an infinitive. What combinations of aspects are possible in such constructions? For some verbs, any possible combination of aspects may be used, the choice being determined by the meaning you wish to convey:

Я хочу́ чита́ть. (I want to read.)
Я хочу́ прочита́ть э́ту кни́гу. (I want to read [finish] this book.)

For others, however, only one aspect is possible. The following verbs can be used as auxiliaries only with **imperfective** infinitives. (The auxiliaries themselves can be either imperfective or perfective, unless only one form is listed.)

начина́ть/нача́ть	to begin
конча́ть/ко́нчить	to end
стать (perf.)	to become
продолжа́ть (imperf.)	to continue
переставать/переста́ть	to stop
привыка́ть/привы́кнуть	to get used (to something)
отвыка́ть/отвы́кнуть	to get unused (to something)
приуча́ть/приучи́ть	to accustom (someone to something)
отуча́ть/отучи́ть	to get someone unaccustomed (to something)
учи́ться/научи́ться	to learn
полюби́ть (perf.)	to love

Са́ша ко́нчил рабо́тать в семь часо́в. (Sasha finished working at seven o'clock.
Мы привы́кли гуля́ть по вечера́м. (We have gotten used to taking walks in the evening.)

The following verbs can be used as auxiliaries only with **perfective** infinitives. (The auxiliaries themselves are all perfective verbs.)

забы́ть	to forget
успе́ть	to do (something) in time
уда́ться	to succeed, manage

Они́ успе́ли пригото́вить у́жин за де́сять мину́т. (They prepared dinner in ten minutes.)

The verbs above do have imperfective forms—забыва́ть, успева́ть, and удава́ться. If these imperfective verbs are used as auxiliaries, the infinitive can be either perfective or imperfective.

Aspect and Negated Infinitives

If an infinitive is negated, it generally is imperfective, even if the perfective was used in the non-negated version of the sentence:

Она́ реши́ла оста́ться в го́роде. (She decided to stay in the city.)
Она́ реши́ла не остава́ться в го́роде. (She decided not to stay in the city.)

If a negated perfective infinitive is used, it indicates a suggestion or warning not to do something accidentally that could cause harm:

Я тебя́ о́чень прошу́ не потеря́ть э́ти де́ньги. (I ask you not to lose this money.)

Aspect and Negated Auxiliaries

If an auxiliary verb is negated and the infinitive is imperfective, the action is not allowed or is inadvisable. If an auxiliary verb is negated and the infinitive is perfective, the action cannot be performed.

Он не мо́жет чита́ть э́ту кни́гу. (He can't read this book. [It's inappropriate reading for him, he's not allowed to read it.])
Он не мо́жет прочита́ть э́ту кни́гу. (He can't read this book. [He's incapable of it, it's too difficult for him.])

If modal expressions are used instead of auxiliary verbs, the same rules apply for aspect:

Не на́до чита́ть э́ту кни́гу. (Don't read this book. [It's not advisable, for one reason or another, to read it.])

Since на́до (it is necessary) is concerned with what is advised, not what is forbidden, the imperfective infinitive is needed here.

§12.5 TENSE

There are three tenses in Russian: past, present, and future. Each tense can be translated into English in several different ways. The choice depends on both aspect and the context. For example, the imperfective past tense form, он чита́л, may be translated as he read, he was reading, he has read, he used to read, or he had been reading. The present tense form, она́ чита́ет, may be translated as she is reading, she reads, or she has been reading. The imperfective future form, они́ бу́дут чита́ть, may be translated as they will read, they will be reading, or they will have read.

§12.5-1 PAST TENSE

The past tense is the easiest to form. It is also different in formation from the other two tenses.

The past tense stem must be used to form the past tense. This stem is obtained, in most cases, by dropping -ть from the infinitive form of the verb: игра́ть → игра- (to play). (It does not matter whether a verb is perfective or imperfective—the same procedure is used.) Then one of the following is added to this stem:

Singular			Plural
Masculine	**Neuter**	**Feminine**	
-л	-ло	-ла	-ли

As you know, in the other tenses, the verb forms differ according to person: я, ты, он, онá, etc. Number also plays a role, as does gender (in the third person singular only). In the past tense, on the other hand, person is irrelevant when it comes to endings, while gender and number are the deciding factors. For example, when using the verb игрáть:

If you need a masculine singular noun, write:
игрáл (for он and masculine я and ты)

If you need a feminine singular noun, write:
игрáла (for онá and feminine я and ты)

If you need a neuter singular noun, write:
игрáло (for онó)

If you need a plural noun, write:
игрáли (for мы, вы, and они)

The formation of the past tense is generally quite simple, but there are some irregular verbs, particularly among those that end in -ти:

	нести (to carry)	везти (to transport by vehicle)	вести (to lead, take along)	расти (to grow)	идти (to walk, go)
он	нёс	вёз	вёл	рос	шёл
онó	неслó	везлó	велó	,рослó	шло
онá	неслá	везлá	велá	рослá	шла
они	несли	везли	вели	росли	шли

Note that several of the masculine singular forms do not have -л, that вести loses the -с-, and that идти may be hard to recognize in the past tense if you do not know that it is irregular.

Verbs whose infinitive stems end in -ере- also lose the -л in the masculine singular. Further, they drop the last -е-:

умерéть (to die)
он ýмер

оно́ у́мерло
она́ умерла́
они́ у́мерли

Verbs that have the suffix -ну- may or may not lose that suffix in the past tense. Most perfective verbs keep it and form the past tense in the regular way. Some perfective verbs do not keep it, and they also do not retain -л in the masculine singular:

дости́гнуть (to achieve)
он дости́г
оно́ дости́гло
она́ дости́гла
они́ дости́гли

привы́кнуть (to get used to [something])
он привы́к
оно́ привы́кло
она́ привы́кла
они́ привы́кли

Most imperfective verbs lose the suffix -ну- and generally also lose -л in the masculine singular:

мёрзнуть (to be chilly, feel cold)
он мёрз
оно́ мёрзло
она́ мёрзла
они́ мёрзли

Verbs that end in -чь use the nonpast stem instead of the past stem to form the past tense. The nonpast stem is formed by removing the ending from the third person plural of the imperfective present or perfective future form:

мочь: они́ мо́г/ут → мог

These verbs do not keep the masculine singular -л.

	мочь (to be able)	**печь** (to bake)	**лечь** (to lie down)	**жечь** (to burn)
он	мог	пёк	лёг	жёг
оно́	могло́	пекло́	легло́	жгло
она́	могла́	пекла́	легла́	жгла
они́	могли́	пекли́	легли́	жгли

Another category of difficult verbs consists of those that end in -сть. Unlike many of the verbs above, they retain -л in the masculine singular, but they do not retain the -с- of the infinitive form:

	сесть (to sit down)	есть (to eat)	класть (to place, put)	упасть (to fall)
он	сел	ел	клал	упа́л
оно́	се́ло	е́ло	кла́ло	упа́ло
она́	се́ла	е́ла	кла́ла	упа́ла
они́	се́ли	е́ли	кла́ли	упа́ли

As you may have noticed, some verbs experience a stress shift in some past tense forms. Generally, most verbs take the same stress as the infinitive. But monosyllabic verbs (verbs with one syllable in the infinitive) are usually stressed on the ending in the feminine singular form. A number of verbs that are not monosyllabic do the same; нача́ть (to begin), заня́ть (to occupy), and prefixed forms of да́ть (to give) also take the stress on the ending in the feminine singular.

нача́ть (to begin): он на́чал, оно́ на́чало, она́ начала́, они́ на́чали

Special Use of the Past Tense
A small number of perfective verbs, most notably пойти́ (to walk, go [on foot]) and пое́хать (to drive, ride, go [by vehicle]), can be used in the past tense to refer to an action that will take place in the future: Ну, мы пошли́. (Well, we are going to go.)

§12.5-2 PRESENT TENSE

There is only one aspect in the present tense, the imperfective, but there are two conjugations. That means that verbs can take one of two possible sets of endings in the present:

	1st Conjugation	**2nd Conjugation**
я	-у	(j) -у
ты	-ешь	-ишь
он, оно́, она́	-ет	-ит
мы	-ем	-им
вы	-ете	-ите
они́	-ут	-ат/-ят

In the first conjugation, е becomes ё when under stress.

As you will see, these conjugations and these endings apply to the perfective future as well. Conjugations do not play a role in the past tense—there is only one set of endings in the past.

The conjugation of a verb will be marked in dictionaries, usually with the Roman numeral I or II. Most first conjugation verbs end in -ать, and most second conjugation verbs end in -ить.

The above endings for the present tense are fairly easy to learn. It is more difficult to determine the form of the stem to which the endings should be added. The past stem, which is formed by removing -ть from the infinitive, generally ends in a vowel. For the present tense, this stem must be changed in some way so that it ends in a consonant. Then the present tense endings can be added. The stem is changed in some verbs by simply removing the vowel. In others, a consonant is added. In some cases, both of these things occur. This stem is the nonpast stem.

First Conjugation Stems

Most first conjugation infinitives end in -ать (-ять) and generally keep the -a- (or -я-). Then the consonant j is added, which softens the vowel that follows:

работать (to work): работа+j → я работа+j+у → я рабо́таю

A number of other first conjugation verbs, ending in еть, also follow this pattern:

боле́ть (to be ill)—я боле́ю

A relatively small group of -ать/-ять verbs loses the -a- (or -я-) and adds the consonant j. This leads to consonant mutation in the final consonant.

Finally, a handful of -ать verbs loses the -a- and does not add j:

ждать (to wait): жд → я жд+у → я жду

(A number of other first conjugation verbs [perfectives ending in -нуть] also follow this pattern in the perfective future: отдохну́ть [to rest]: он отдохнёт.)

Some verbs of this type have an inserted vowel:

брать (to take): бр → я б/е/р+у → я беру́

Second Conjugation Stems

Most second conjugation infinitives end in -ить, and they generally lose the -и-:

любить (to love): люб → мы люб+им → мы любим

Some, but not many, second conjugation verbs end in -еть or -ать. They also lose the vowels that come before the infinitive ending -ть.

Generally, consonant mutation occurs in the first person singular in the second conjugation. (See the chart on consonant mutation in the appendix.) However, the letters ж, ч, ш, and щ do not mutate. The letters н, л, and р do not mutate but do become soft. (You may have noticed the presence of a j in the chart of second conjugation verb endings. It is the cause of this mutation or softness.)

видеть (to see): я вижу, ты видишь
любить (to love): я люблю, ты любишь

Irregular Verbs

Quite a large number of verbs depart from the patterns above in one way or another. Nevertheless, it is still worth learning the rules. After that, it is necessary to learn some verbs individually. Some of the more commonly used exceptional verbs are listed below. A book such as *201 Russian Verbs* by Patricia Davis (Barron's) will provide many more.

Verbs with -давать, -знавать, or -ставать and the unprefixed verb давать lose the suffix -ва- in all forms of the present tense:

	давать (to give)	узнавать (to find out, recognize)	вставать (to get up, stand up)
я	даю	узнаю	встаю
ты	даёшь	узнаёшь	встаёшь
он, оно, она	даёт	узнаёт	встаёт
мы	даём	узнаём	встаём
вы	даёте	узнаёте	встаёте
они	дают	узнают	встают

Verbs with the suffix -ова- (-ева-) in the infinitive lose that suffix in the present tense. -у/-ю is added before the personal endings:

	тре́бовать (to demand)	танцева́ть (to dance)
я	тре́бую	танцу́ю
ты	тре́буешь	танцу́ешь
он, оно́, она́	тре́бует	танцу́ет
мы	тре́буем	танцу́ем
вы	тре́буете	танцу́ете
они́	тре́буют	танцу́ют

The first conjugation verbs пить (to drink), лить (to pour [liquid]), шить (to sew), and бить (to hit) lose the -и and gain a soft sign in the present tense. The verb брить (to shave), however, loses the -и and gains -е. Брить is listed in the chart below, as is пить; all the other verbs in this category follow the pattern of пить and are not listed.

	пить (to drink)	брить (to shave)
я	пью	бре́ю
ты	пьёшь	бре́ешь
он, оно́, она́	пьёт	бре́ет
мы	пьём	бре́ем
вы	пьёте	бре́ете
они́	пьют	бре́ют

The verb пить (to drink) should not be confused with the verb петь (to sing). Although similar in the infinitive, they are quite different not only in meaning but also in the present tense forms. The verb мыть is similar to петь in the present tense, but note the difference in stress:

	петь (to sing)	мыть (to wash)
я	пою	мо́ю
ты	поёшь	мо́ешь
он, оно́, она́	поёт	мо́ет
мы	поём	мо́ем
вы	поёте	мо́ете
они́	пою́т	мо́ют

Жить (to live), while similar to пить (to drink) in the infinitive form, differs from it in the present tense forms. The verb плыть (to swim, float, sail) follows the pattern of жить:

	ЖИТЬ (to live)	ПЛЫТЬ (to swim, float, sail)
я	живу́	плыву́
ты	живёшь	плывёшь
он, оно́, она́	живёт	плывёт
мы	живём	плывём
вы	живёте	плывёте
они́	живу́т	плыву́т

If you know only the infinitive, жить may be hard to recognize in its present tense forms. The verbs éхать (to go, ride, drive) and есть (to eat) are even more difficult to recognize:

	ёхать (to go, ride, drive)	есть (to eat)
я	ёду	ем
ты	ёдешь	ешь
он, онó, онá	ёдет	ест
мы	ёдем	едúм
вы	ёдете	едúте
онú	ёдут	едя́т

Do not confuse the infinitive есть (to eat) with есть, the third person singular form of быть (to be). Note that the infinitives ёхать and есть have similar plural forms: only the endings (and the stress) distinguish the two verbs in the plural.

Ехать takes first conjugation endings, while есть takes second conjugation endings.

Verbs that end in -чь have a few complications in the present tense forms:

	мочь (to be able)	печь (to bake)	жечь (to burn)
я	могý	пекý	жгу
ты	мóжешь	печёшь	жжешь
он, онó, онá	мóжет	печёт	жжёт
мы	мóжем	печём	жжём
вы	мóжете	печёте	жжёте
онú	мóгут	пекýт	жгут

Pay attention to the consonant alternation. It can be either г/ж (as it is here for мочь and жечь), or к/ч (as it is here for печь). Note the consistency in the alternation: the first person singular and third person plural take the first consonant (г or к) and the other forms take the second consonant (ж or ч).

Some verbs that end in -сти also have special problems:

	вести (to lead, take along)	**расти** (to grow)
я	веду́	расту́
ты	ведёшь	растёшь
он, оно́, она́	ведёт	растёт
мы	ведём	растём
вы	ведёте	растёте
они́	веду́т	расту́т

Another verb, one which ends in -сть, should be noted here as well:

класть (to place)
я кладу́
ты кладёшь
он, оно́, она́ кладёт
мы кладём
вы кладёте
они́ кладу́т

There are two verbs that are so irregular that they have endings from both the first conjugation and the second conjugation:

	хоте́ть (to want)	**бежа́ть** (to run)
я	хочу́	бегу́
ты	хо́чешь	бежи́шь
он, оно́, она́	хо́чет	бежи́т
мы	хоти́м	бежи́м
вы	хоти́те	бежи́те
они́	хотя́т	бегу́т

Nothing is regular in хотéть. The singular forms of the verb have first conjugation endings, while the plural forms belong to the second conjugation. The consonant mutation is also unusual. Ordinarily, consonant mutation occurs either in the first person singular or in all six forms of a verb. Here it occurs in the three singular forms. The stress patterns are equally unusual in that the stress shifts back to the end of the verb for all the plural forms (see "Stress in Present Tense Verbs," below).

In бежáть, the third person plural form belongs to the first conjugation, while the other forms are of the second conjugation. Note that the consonant alternation in this verb is identical to the alternation in another exceptional verb, мочь: г/ж.

Stress in Present Tense Verbs

As a general rule, stress is stable in the present tense. The same stress applies as in the infinitive. But it may shift if, in the infinitive, it falls on a vowel that drops out in the formation of the present tense. Stress shift does not occur in all verbs of this type, but when it does, it affects all forms except the first person singular.

For example, in спешúть (to hurry) and просúть (to ask), the stressed vowel falls out in the formation of the present tense. Stress shift does not occur in the first verb, but it does in the second:

	спешúть (to hurry)	просúть (to ask)
я	спешý	прошý
ты	спешúшь	прóсишь
он, онó, онá	спешит	прóсит
мы	спешúм	прóсим
вы	спешúте	прóсите
онú	спешáт	прóсят

Special Uses of the Present Tense

The present tense can be used to refer to an action that has taken place in the past:

Сегóдня ýтром я открывáю дверь и вѝжу большýю, злýю собáку.
(This morning I opened the door and saw a big, angry dog.)

The context (сегóдня ýтром) makes it clear that the event actually took place in the past. Such usage of the present tense provides immediacy and increases the emotional power of the statement.

The present tense may also be used to refer to an action that will take place in the future:

Зáвтра мы éдем в гóрод. (Tomorrow we're going to the city.)

Again, the context (зáвтра) makes it clear that the event will actually take place in the future. Such usage of the present tense indicates that the speaker is certain that the action will take place as stated. The use of the present tense when referring to the future is not common and occurs most frequently with determinate verbs of motion. Indeterminate verbs of motion are not used. (See §12.11 for an explanation of verbs of motion.)

§12.5-3 FUTURE TENSE

In contrast to the present tense, which has only the imperfective aspect, the future tense has two aspects, the perfective and the imperfective. As a result, there are two future verb forms: the imperfective future and the perfective future. The **imperfective future** is quite easy to form, even though it is a compound verb.

The verb быть (to be) is used as an auxiliary:

быть (to be)
  я бýду
  ты бýдешь
  он, онó, онá бýдет
  мы бýдем
  вы бýдете
  онѝ бýдут

It is followed by an imperfective verb in the infinitive form.

Я бýду отдыхáть. (I'm going to rest.)
Вы бýдете ýжинать? (Will you be having dinner?)

To form the **perfective future,** the same endings are used as in the present tense:

	1st Conjugation	**2nd Conjugation**
я	-у	(j) -у
ты	-ешь	-ишь
он, онó, онá	-ет	-ит
мы	-ем	-им ·
вы	-ете	-ите
онй	-ут	-ат/-ят

(In the first conjugation, e becomes ё when under stress.)

In the present, however, these endings are added to imperfective verbs, because only imperfective verbs have a present tense. In the perfective future, these endings are added to perfective verbs. Compare:

Онá читáет кнúгу. (She is reading the book.)
Онá прочитáет кнúгу. (She will read the book.)

Although these two verbs are quite similar in *form*, they are not the same and should not be confused. The first one is a present tense imperfective verb, the second is a future tense perfective verb.

This perfective verb, like many others, is formed by adding a prefix to an imperfective verb. Such verb pairs differ in form only in the prefix, take the same endings, and belong to the same conjugation. Not all verb pairs are so similar, however, and some do not even belong to the same conjugation. In the verb pair получáть/получúть (to receive), for example, the imperfective verb belongs to the first conjugation, while the perfective one is of the second conjugation:

	получа́ть (to receive) imperfective aspect present tense	получи́ть (to receive) perfective aspect future tense
я	получа́ю	получу́
ты	получа́ешь	полу́чишь
он, оно́, она́	получа́ет	полу́чит
мы	получа́ем	полу́чим
вы	получа́ете	полу́чите
они́	получа́ют	полу́чат

Verb Stems

As in the present tense, you must determine the form of the stem to which verb endings are added in the perfective future. The same principles apply as in the present tense. See "First Conjugation Stems" and "Second Conjugation Stems" in §12.5-2.

Irregular Verbs

The verb мочь (to be able) does not have an imperfective future form. The prefixed perfective forms of the imperfective irregular verbs given in §12.5-2 are like their imperfective counterparts in every respect except the prefix. For this reason, they are not listed again here. (Compare: танцева́ть [to dance]—я танцу́ю and потанцева́ть [to dance]—я потанцу́ю.)

In general, stress remains the same when a prefix is added to a verb (see "Stress in Present Tense Verbs" in §12.5-2), but if the prefix is вы- and the verb is perfective, then the stress shifts to the prefix.

In some verbs, the imperfective present and the perfective future verb forms differ only in stress:

	узнавáть (to find out, recognize) imperfective aspect present tense	узнáть (to find out, recognize) perfective aspect future tense
я	узнаю́	узнáю
ты	узнаёшь	узнáешь
он, онó, онá	узнаёт	узнáет
мы	узнаём	узнáем
вы	узнаёте	узнáете
они́	узнаю́т	узнáют

(Note that the stress in the imperfective form turns е to ё.)
Compare: узнавáть/узнáть and разрезáть/разрéзать (to cut up) from "The Formation of the Aspects" in §12.4. In the case of разрезáть/разрéзать, it is the infinitives that differ only in stress, not the personal verb forms. With узнавáть/узнáть, it is the other way around.

Of course, not all perfective verbs are formed by simply adding a prefix to an imperfective verb. Some have their own forms and some of those forms are irregular.

As you may remember, the imperfective verbs давáть (to give), узнавáть (to find out, recognize), and вставáть (to get up, stand up) are irregular, as are their perfective counterparts. Узнáть appears above. The others are given below, and начáть (to begin) is also included with this group.

	дать (to give)	встать (to get up, stand up)	начáть (to begin)
я	дам	встáну	начнý
ты	дашь	встáнешь	начнёшь
он, онó, онá	даст	встáнет	начнёт
мы	дадúм	встáнем	начнём
вы	дадúте	встáнете	начнёте
они́	дадýт	встáнут	начнýт

As was mentioned in §12.5-1, verbs whose infinitive stems end in -ере- are irregular in the past tense. They are also irregular in the future: they lose the first -е-.

умере́ть (to die)
  я умру́
  ты умрёшь
  он, оно́, она́ умрёт
  мы умрём
  вы умрёте
  они́ умру́т

Special attention should be paid to the verb взять (to take) and verbs that end in -нять (поня́ть [to understand], приня́ть [to accept]):

	взять (to take)	поня́ть (to understand)	приня́ть (to accept)
я	возьму́	пойму́	приму́
ты	возьмёшь	поймёшь	при́мешь
он, оно́, она́	возьмёт	поймёт	при́мет
мы	возьмём	поймём	при́мем
вы	возьмёте	поймёте	при́мете
они́	возьму́т	пойму́т	при́мут

As you might expect, verbs that end in -чь present some problems. The verb лечь (to lie down) in the perfective future follows the pattern of the present tense forms of the imperfective verb жечь (to burn):

лечь (to lie down)
  я ля́гу
  ты ля́жешь
  он, оно́, она́ ля́жет
  мы ля́жем
  вы ля́жете
  они́ ля́гут

You have seen in the other tenses that verbs ending in -сть can be difficult. This does not change in the future tense:

	сесть (to sit down)	упа́сть (to fall)
я	ся́ду	упаду́
ты	ся́дешь	упадёшь
он, оно́, она́	ся́дет	упадёт
мы	ся́дем	упадём
вы	ся́дете	упадёте
они́	ся́дут	упаду́т

Special Uses of the Future Tense

The future tense can be used to refer to an action that has taken place in the past:

> Быва́ло, что она́ позвони́т и́ли придёт. (It used to happen that she would call or drop by.)

The context (быва́ло) makes it clear that the event actually took place in the past. Such usage of the future tense indicates a recurring action in the past.

The future tense may also be used to refer to an action that is taking place in the present:

> По́сле обе́да я ма́ло де́лаю. Я пойду́ за хле́бом и зайду́ за молоко́м. (After lunch I don't do much. I'll go get some bread and stop in for milk.)

The first sentence makes it clear that the event is actually taking place in the present. Such usage of the future tense indicates a recurring or habitual action in the present.

In addition, the future tense can indicate general ability:

> Они́ э́то сде́лают. (They can do that.)

Such a statement does not refer to future action, but rather to present capabilities.

Only the perfective future is used in the special uses of the future tense that are given above.

§12.6 THE INFINITIVE

The infinitive is a verb form that expresses neither tense nor person, but simply names the verb: игра́ть (to play), ждать (to wait).

Because an infinitive is so general, it is the form in which verbs appear in the dictionary. Russian infinitives translated into English are preceded by the word "to":

сидéть—to sit

The infinitives of Russian verbs usually come in pairs: one infinitive of the pair is imperfective, the other is perfective (читáть/почитáть [to read]). The imperfective form is usually listed first in dictionaries, glossaries, and textbooks.

Most Russian infinitives end in -ть, but some end in -чь or -ти. Some verbs have the particle -ся in addition to one of these endings (занимáться—to study); they are discussed in §12.10.

The stem obtained from the infinitive is often called the past stem because it is used to form the past tense. It is also used to form some participles (see §12.13). The past stem is formed by dropping the infinitive ending:

рабóтать → рабóта- (to work)

All infinitives that end in -ти are stressed on -ти (идти́— to walk). All infinitives that end in -чь are stressed on the last syllable (помóчь—to help). Infinitives that end in -ть do not follow a predictable stress pattern; the stress can fall on any syllable in the verb (бéгать [to run], готóвить [to prepare], изучáть [to study]).

In sentences, infinitives can be combined with auxiliary verbs, modal expressions, some short-form adjectives, some adverbs, and some nouns.

1. AUXILIARY VERBS
Infinitives are used with auxiliary verbs in a number of ways. They may be used for:

Motion for a Stated Purpose

Мы éздили отдыхáть в дерéвню. (We went to [get some] rest in the countryside.)

Beginning, End, or Continuation of Action

Он нáчал рабóтать. (He started to work.)

Attitude to Action

Я хочý танцевáть. (I want to dance.)
Они́ лю́бят собирáть грибы́. (They like to collect mushrooms.)

Call to Action

Я вас прошý прийти́ зáвтра. (Please come tomorrow. [I ask you to come tomorrow.])

Ability to Perform Action

Она́ мо́жет пое́хать в го́род за́втра. (She can go to the city tomorrow.)
Ни́на уме́ет чита́ть. (Nina can read.)

Note: 1. Although both мочь and уме́ть indicate ability to perform an action, уме́ть refers to the ability to exercise a learned skill.

2. Знать (to know) cannot be used directly with an infinitive:

Я зна́ю, как прое́хать на да́чу. (I know how to get to the dacha.)

2. MODAL EXPRESSIONS
Modal expressions must be used with infinitives:

Мне на́до прочита́ть э́ту статью́. (I need to read this article.)
Нам необходи́мо поговори́ть. (It is necessary for us to talk.)

For more on this subject, including the use of the past and future with modal expressions, see the section on modal expressions in §9.3-5, the Dative Case.

3. SHORT-FORM ADJECTIVES
Infinitives can be used with some short-form adjectives, most notably with рад (happy) and гото́в (ready):

Мы ра́ды вас ви́деть. (We're happy to see you.)
Он всегда́ гото́в помо́чь. (He's always ready to help.)

For the past or future tense, add forms of the verb быть:

Мы бу́дем ра́ды вас ви́деть. (We'll be happy to see you.)
Он всегда́ был гото́в помо́чь. (He was always ready to help.)

4. ADVERBS
Infinitives can be used with some predicate adverbs, most notably:

интере́сно	interesting
легко́	easy
тру́дно	difficult
ску́чно	boring
гру́стно	sad
ве́село	cheerful
прия́тно	pleasant

Ему́ тру́дно реши́ть э́ту зада́чу. (It's difficult for him to solve this problem.)
Нам гру́стно уезжа́ть. (It's sad for us to leave.)

Note that the person performing the action in the sentence is in the dative case.

For the past or future tense, add forms of the verb быть:

Ему́ бу́дет тру́дно реши́ть э́ту зада́чу. (It will be difficult for him to solve this problem.)
Нам бы́ло гру́стно уезжа́ть. (It was sad for us to leave.)

For more on adverbs, see §13.

5. NOUNS

As you have seen above, certain verbs, adjectives, and adverbs are used with infinitives. Nouns that have the same roots as these words, or are very similar in meaning to them, can also be used with infinitives:

У меня к вам просьба не курить. (Please don't smoke.)
Compare: Я вас прошу не курить. (Please don't smoke.)

Он высказал готовность помочь. (He expressed a readiness to help.)
Compare: Он всегда готов помочь. (He's always ready to help.)

The verb хотеть (to want) cannot be turned into a noun with the same root, so желание (desire) is used instead:

Они выразили желание это сделать. (They expressed the desire to do that.)
Compare: Они хотят это сделать. (They want to do that.)

§12.7 AUXILIARY VERBS

In Russian, the only tense that requires an auxiliary verb is the imperfective future. Future tense forms of быть (to be) are used as auxiliaries for an infinitive:

быть (to be)
я буду
ты будешь
он, оно, она будет
мы будем
вы будете
они будут

Я буду говорить. (I will speak.)
Мы будем ужинать. (We will have dinner.)

Auxiliary verbs are also used when the meaning of the sentence calls for them. Certain categories of action need to be described by means of an auxiliary verb and an infinitive. A statement about the ability to perform an action, a call to action, an expression of an attitude toward an action, the beginning, end, or continuation of an action, or a motion performed for a stated purpose generally require an auxiliary verb and an infinitive:

Мы можем приехать сегодня. (We can come today.)
Они просят нас уйти. (They're asking us to leave.)
Он хочет обедать. (He wants to have lunch.)
Студенты кончили заниматься. (The students finished studying.)
Дети ходили играть в парке. (The children went to play in the park.)

See also the section on infinitives and auxiliary verbs in §12.6.

12.8
THE FORMA-
TION OF THE
IMPERATIVE

The imperative can end in -и or have a zero ending. In the plural/formal variant of the imperative, -те is added. A multi-step process must be followed to determine which ending should be added to a particular verb:

   1. The nonpast stem of a verb is used to form the imperative (the same stem that is used to form the present tense). To obtain the nonpast stem, remove the ending from the third person plural form (use the present tense for imperfective verbs, and the perfective future tense for perfective verbs).

> говори́ть (to speak): они говор/я́т → говор-
> чита́ть (to read): они чита/ют → они чита+j+ут → чита+j-
> встать (to get up): они встан/ут → встан-

(For more on the formation of the nonpast stem, see §12.5-2.)

   2. If the nonpast stem ends in a vowel + j, then the imperative will have a zero ending in the singular and a zero ending + те in the plural. Since it is located after a vowel, the -j at the end of the stem will be spelled й:

> чита́й/чита́йте (read)

Some textbooks list such endings as -й/-йте, but because the nonpast stem of verbs with this ending ends in -j, it would be more correct to say it is -/-те.

   3. If the nonpast stem ends in a consonant other than j, an intermediate step must be taken before adding the imperative endings. Look at the stress of the first person singular of the verb in the nonpast:

> говори́ть— говор- : я говорю́
> встать— встан- : я вста́ну

   4. If the stress in the first person singular falls on the ending (or on any syllable other than the second-to-last syllable), then the imperative endings will be -и/-ите:

> говори́! / говори́те! (speak!)

   5. If the stress of the first person singular falls on the second-to-last syllable, then the imperative endings will be -/-те. The -и imperative ending fell out for these verbs, but the softness of the consonant marked by that vowel remains. As a result, there is a soft sign at the end of such imperatives: встань! / вста́ньте! (get up!). Some textbooks list these endings as -ь/-ьте.

The stress of the first person singular is important not only for determining the form of the imperative, but because the imperative will take the same stress:

я говорю— говори/говорите   (end stress)
я встану— встань/встаньте   (stem stress)

Exceptions

1. If the nonpast stem of a verb ends in two consonants, then the imperative form of that verb will end in -и/-ите, regardless of stress:

кри́кнуть (to shout): [я кри́кну]— кри́кни/кри́кните

2. Verbs that end in -давать, -знавать, and -ставать do not lose -ва- in the formation of the imperative. These imperatives have a zero ending:

узнава́ть (to [try to] find out): узнава+j- → узнава́й/узнава́йте

3. The prefixed and unprefixed forms of дать are irregular in their formation:

дать (to give): [они даду́т]— дай/да́йте

4. Monosyllabic verbs ending in -ить form the imperative according to the following pattern:

пить (to drink): [они пьют]— пей/пе́йте

5. Лечь (to lie down) and the unprefixed and prefixed forms of есть (to eat) form their imperatives irregularly:

лечь (to lie down): [они ля́гут]— ляг/ля́гте
есть (to eat): [они едя́т]— ешь/е́шьте

6. Éхать (to drive) does not form an imperative. Use поезжа́й (-те).

Some verbs do not have imperatives. The meaning of these verbs excludes the possibility of imperative forms:

хоте́ть   to want
мочь   to be able
ви́деть   to see
слы́шать   to hear

A person cannot be commanded, for example, to want or to hear. (He or she may, however, be commanded to listen: слу́шай—слу́шайте.)

The Imperative and Aspect

In both the imperfective and the perfective aspect, imperatives refer to the future. They express a request or a demand for action in the immediate or distant future:

Пойди́ в магази́н. (Go to the store.)
Отвеча́й на вопро́с. (Answer the question.)

The imperfective aspect is used when the speaker does not wish or need to emphasize results, but is simply requesting the performance of an action:

Сиди́ здесь. (Sit here.)
Де́ти, игра́йте в саду́. (Children, play in the yard.)

It is also used for habitual actions:

Клади́те ста́рые газе́ты сюда́. (Put old newspapers here.)

The perfective aspect is used when the speaker wishes to emphasize results:

Дай мне слова́рь. (Give me the dictionary.)
Прочита́йте письмо́. (Read the letter.)

The speaker is not interested in the process involved in these actions, but wants the dictionary in hand and the letter to be read.

The perfective may also be used when an action is so brief that process cannot be an issue:

Закро́й дверь. (Close the door.)

If a request is made (via the imperative or in some other way) and it is not fulfilled, then the request may be repeated. If repeated (and if an imperative is used), it will be in the form of an imperfective imperative, regardless of the aspect used in the original request. This use of the imperfective carries with it the connotation "go ahead, get on with it":

—Отве́ть на вопро́с. ("Answer the question.")
—Что тако́е? Отвеча́й! ("What's the matter? Answer!")

Negated imperatives are generally imperfective. The negated perfective imperative has a special, limited use—it serves as a warning not to do something that may have negative consequences:

Не забу́дь ему́ позвони́ть. (Don't forget to call him.)

Such sentences may start with the imperative смотри́ (-те) (watch it, watch out), which makes the warning stronger:

Смотри́, не забу́дь ему́ позвони́ть.

Special Use of the Infinitive as Imperative
The infinitive may sometimes be used as an imperative, but only as a very strong command, never as a request or a

suggestion. It is generally used only by superiors to their subordinates. Most often it implies anger or urgency:

Встать!   Get up!
Молчáть!   Silence!

The First Person Imperative

Another kind of imperative is used when the speaker wants to include him- or herself. Instead of saying "[you] do this," the speaker says "let's do this [together]."

The Imperfective First Person Imperative
   1. Use давáй if you are speaking to one person with whom you use ты. (See §8 for more on forms of address.) Use давáйте if you are speaking to two or more people, or if you are speaking to one person with whom you use вы. (See §8 for more on forms of address.)
   2. Add давáй or давáйте to an imperfective infinitive:

Давáй танцевáть.   Let's dance.
Давáйте обéдать.   Let's have lunch.

The Perfective First Person Imperative
   1. With perfective verbs, the use of давáй/давáйте is optional.
   2. Add давáй or давáйте, if you are using it, to the first person plural form of the perfective verb:

Давáй поéдем в гóрод.   (Let's go to the city.)
Приготóвим ýжин.   (Let's prepare dinner.)

Note that мы is not used in such constructions.

The Third Person Imperative

In this kind of imperative, the speaker requires something from someone for another person or persons. The third person imperative may also imply, "I don't care whether he/she does that. Let him/her do it."
   This imperative is very easy to form. The word пусть (let) (or, in colloquial usage, пускáй) is placed at the front of the sentence. No new verb forms are required, and the verb agrees with the subject, which is usually included:

Пусть онá отдыхáет. (Let her rest.)

Sometimes the subject is understood to be present:

Пусть игрáют. (Let [them] play.)

Perfective or imperfective aspect may be used in the third person imperative. The choice will be based on what you want to say. If you are interested in process, for example, you will use the imperfective. Follow the guidelines for aspect in §12.4.

§12.9 THE FORMA-TION OF THE CONDITIONAL

As stated in §12.3-3, the conditional is used to indicate an action that could have occurred (but did not), or may occur under certain (possible or impossible) circumstances.

The conditional is fairly easy to form.

1. For actions that could have occurred but did not, the particle бы is needed. Бы sometimes appears in the abbreviated form, б, but other than that it does not change in form. The verbs in the sentence are always in the past tense:

> Если бы мы пришли раньше, мы бы успели на поезд. (If we had come earlier, we would have been in time for the train.)

The clause which states the condition that would have made the action possible (earlier arrival at the station) begins with если (if). The particle бы in that clause must immediately follow если. The particle бы in the other clause may occur in a number of positions in the clause, but it is generally found in the second position or after the verb. It cannot come first in the clause. The clause that begins with если may appear either first or second in the sentence:

> Мы бы успели на поезд, если бы мы пришли раньше.

The same kind of construction can be used to refer to future events, provided that they are unrealistic or impossible:

> Если бы я стала президентом страны, я бы исправила экономику. (If I became president of the country, I would improve the economy.)

For other statements that refer to the future, the guidelines in #2, below, apply.

2. For actions that may reasonably occur, если is used and бы is not used. The verbs in the sentence are in the future tense:

> Если я буду в магазине сегодня, я куплю молоко. (If I am in the store today, I will buy milk.)

The clause which states the condition that will make the action possible (being in the store) begins with если. The clause with если may be either first or second in the sentence:

> Я куплю молоко, если я буду в магазине.

In both kinds of conditional sentences, perfective or imperfective aspect may be used. The choice will be based on what you want to say. If you are interested in actions as processes, for example, you will use imperfective. Follow the guidelines on aspect in §12.4.

The Use of бы *to Express Wishes or Requests*
All the examples above consist of sentences with two clauses. Бы can also be used in sentences with a single clause. Such sentences express a wish or a request. A wish can refer to the future or to the past (in other words, to a lost opportunity). All verbs in such constructions, however, are in the past tense, whether they refer to the past or future. The particle бы is generally found in the second position:

Я бы поéхала в Парѝж.	I would like to go to Paris.
Ты бы э́того не дéлал.	You shouldn't do that.

Хорошó (good) or нáдо (it is necessary) can be used in sentences of a similar type. Several changes take place in the sentence structure as a result. There is no subject, the verb takes the infinitive form, and бы́ло (the neuter singular past tense form of the verb "to be") may be added. The result is an impersonal sentence in which the speaker expresses a general wish that seemingly applies to everyone, rather than a personal desire that applies only to him- or herself:

Хорошó (бы́ло) бы поéхать в Парѝж.	It would be good to go to Paris.
Нáдо (бы́ло) бы поéхать в Парѝж.	It is necessary to go to Paris.

In such sentences, бы is also in the second position.

Wishes Expressed by the Use of хотéть
Of course, a wish can also be expressed without the use of бы:

Я хочý поéхать в Парѝж. (I want to go to Paris.)

But such a sentence can sound a bit forceful or blunt. By adding бы you can keep хотéть and still make the statement diplomatic and mild:

Я бы хотéла поéхать в Парѝж. (I would like to go to Paris.)

Note the change of the verb to past tense, obligatory in sentences with бы.

§12.10 VERBS THAT END IN -СЯ

Quite a number of verbs can be used with -ся. -Ся is placed at the end of a verb and does not cause any other changes in its form. When added to a verb form that ends in a vowel, it takes the form -сь.

	открыва́ть (to open)	открыва́ться (to open)
я	открыва́ю	открыва́юсь
ты	открыва́ешь	открыва́ешься
он, оно́, она́	открыва́ет	открыва́ется
мы	открыва́ем	открыва́емся
вы	открыва́ете	открыва́етесь
они́	открыва́ют	открыва́ются

Why add -ся to a verb? In order to make it intransitive. All verbs that end in -ся are intransitive—they cannot have an accusative direct object. Use the version of the verb with ся when the sentence has no direct object. Compare, for example, the transitive verb закры́ть (to close) and the intransitive verb закры́ться (to close):

| Он закры́л дверь. | He closed the door. |
| Магазин закры́лся. | The store closed. |

Some verbs with -ся are reflexive: the action of the verb is performed by the subject upon the subject.

| | Он мо́ется. | He's washing (reflexive) |
| Compare: | Он мо́ет пол. | He's washing the floor. (not reflexive) |

Although most verbs can be used either with or without -ся, some always have to have -ся:

боя́ться	to be afraid
каза́ться	to seem
улыба́ться	to smile
смея́ться	to laugh
наде́яться	to hope
станови́ться	to become

§12.11 VERBS OF MOTION

As you have seen, Russian verbs fall into two aspect categories, imperfective and perfective. Verbs of motion are further broken down into the categories of determinate and indeterminate. The most common verbs of motion are:

Determinate	Indeterminate	
идти́	ходи́ть	to walk, go (on foot)
бежа́ть	бе́гать	to run
е́хать	е́здить	to drive, ride, go (by vehicle)
лете́ть	лета́ть	to fly
плыть	пла́вать	to swim, sail, float
нести́	носи́ть	to carry (when walking)
вести́	води́ть	to lead, take along (when walking)
везти́	вози́ть	to transport (by vehicle)

(Remember that идти́, нести́, вести́, and везти́ are irregular in the past, вести́ is irregular in the present, and е́хать is irregular in the present and the imperative. See §12.5 and §12.8.)

All the verbs given in the chart above are imperfective. What, then, distinguishes them? Determinate verbs describe motion in a single direction that occurs only once on a given occasion:

$$\longrightarrow$$

Indeterminate verbs describe motion in more than one direction or motion which occurs more than once:

Ма́ша идёт в магази́н. (Masha is going to the store.)

One action in a single direction—determinate verb

Дéти бéгают в пáрке. (The children are running around in the park.)

Action in many directions—indeterminate verb

Эти грузовикú вóзят хлеб. (These trucks transport bread.)

Action that occurs more than once—indeterminate verb

Ваш ребёнок хóдит?   (Does your baby walk [yet]?)

Action in general—indeterminate verb

Вчерá мы éздили в гóрод. (Yesterday we went to the city.)

Round trip, action in more than one direction—indeterminate verb

The meaning of вестú/водúть may present a problem. It describes the action of walking and simultaneously taking someone along who is also walking:

Мы ведём детéй в парк. (We are taking the children to the park.)

It should not be confused with везтú/возúть (to transport [by vehicle]), which looks very much like it. See §12.5 for charts of these verbs. Note that they have irregularities in their forms.

Вестú/водúть has a special use that may seem somewhat peculiar, given that it generally refers to motion on foot: it is the verb pair used when referring to the process of driving a vehicle or the ability to drive a vehicle:

Свéта умéет водúть автомобúль. (Sveta knows how to drive a car.)

When using везтú/возúть, the following distinction should be kept in mind: use везтú/возúть when referring to the transportation of someone or something in a vehicle. Use éхать/éздить when referring to driving or riding in a vehicle. In other words, the first verb pair is transitive and the second verb pair is intransitive:

Кáждый день, Кúра вóзит Пáвла на рабóту. (Every day Kira drives Pavel to work.)
Онú éздят на рабóту. (They drive to work.)

One special use of идтú/ходúть may cause confusion. If you are describing the motion of a vehicle other than a car, taxi, airplane, or helicopter, you generally use идтú/ходúть:

Пóезд шёл бúстро. (The train was going fast.)
Троллéйбус идёт в центр гóрода (The trolley is going to the center of town.)

(Although you should know this rule, you will see it broken on occasion in actual practice. Éхать/éздить also occurs in such sentences.) Keep in mind that идти/ходить is used in this context only when the vehicle is the subject of the sentence. When people or things traveling in these vehicles are the subjects, then it does not apply:

> Мы éдем на троллéйбусе в центр гóрода. (We're going to the center of town on the trolley.)

Prefixes and Verbs of Motion

The categories of determinate and indeterminate apply only to unprefixed verbs of motion. When prefixes are added to these verbs, only the categories of perfective and imperfective apply.

When a prefix is added to a determinate verb, the new verb is perfective. When a prefix is added to an indeterminate verb, in most cases the new verb is imperfective.

Some verbs experience a change in the stem when a prefix is added:

> éздить → -езжáть (for example, приезжáть)
> идти → -йти (for example, зайти)

A stress shift occurs in prefixed forms of бéгать (прибегáть, забегáть). For prefixed forms of éхать/éздить, the hard sign must be added after the prefix if the prefix ends in a consonant: съéхать, въезжáть. For prefixed forms of идти, -о must be added after the prefix if the prefix ends in a consonant: войти. No imperfective verbs are formed by adding a prefix to плáвать.

The following is a list of the most common prefixes used with verbs of motion and their general meanings:

в-   movement into an enclosed space

> Онá вбежáла в дом. (She ran into the house.)

вы-   movement out of an enclosed space

> Онá выбежала из дóма. (She ran out of the house.)

при-   arrival at a place or the bringing of something to a place

> Он пришёл к нам в гóсти и принёс цветы. (He came to visit us and brought flowers.)

у-   departure from a place or the removal of something from a place

> Они уéхали из гóрода. (They left the city.)

за-   1. stopping at a place on the way to some-
                               where else

Мы заéхали в магазúн, чтóбы купúть молокó. (We dropped into the
   store to buy some milk.)

                             2. movement behind a person or object

Ребёнок забежáл за дверь. (The child ran behind the door.)

до-   movement to a location, object, or person

Дéти дошлú до шкóлы. (The children reached the school.)

от-   movement away from a location, object, or
                             person, or the removal of someone or
                             something away from a location, object, or
                             person

Áня отошлá от окнá. (Anya walked away from the window.)
Сáша отвёл ребёнка от лéстницы. (Sasha led the child away from the
   staircase.)

вз- (вс-)   movement upward

Птúцы взлетáют на высóкие дерéвья. (The birds fly up onto the tall
   trees.)

с   1. movement downward

Птúцы слетáют с высóких дерéвьев. (The birds fly down from the tall
   trees.)

                             2. the gathering of people or objects from
                             many locations into one location (when
                             used with this prefix in this meaning, verbs
                             require the addition of -ся)

Все съéхались на собрáние. (Everyone gathered for the meeting.)

раз- (рас-)   the scattering of people or objects from
                             one location to many locations (when used
                             with this prefix in this meaning, verbs
                             require the addition of -ся)

Все разошлúсь пóсле собрáния (Everyone dispersed after the
   meeting.)

под-   approach up to a location, person, or object

Лóдка подплылá к бéрегу. (The boat approached the shore.)

пере-   movement from one location to another, or
                             movement across something

Мы перейдём чéрез ýлицу на углý. (We'll cross the street at the
   corner.)

про- movement past or through a location, or movement covering a set distance

Он прохо́дит ми́мо э́того магази́на ка́ждый день. (He walks past this store every day.)
Он прохо́дит че́рез э́тот парк ка́ждый день. (He walks through this park every day.)
Он прохо́дит ми́лю ка́ждый день. (He walks a mile every day.)

об- movement around a person or object, or movement to various locations in sequence

Де́ти обошли́ весь дом. (The children walked around the entire house.)
Мы объе́хали все магази́ны. (We went around to all the stores.)

(Note the variety of prepositions in the sentences above. For a discussion of prepositions, see §15.)

The most common prefix is по-, which does not have as clear-cut a meaning as the prefixes above. When used with determinate verbs, it sometimes indicates the beginning of an action:

Пти́цы полете́ли на юг. (The birds flew off to the south.)

More often, however, по- acts as a general-purpose prefix that carries no special added meaning:

Мы пойдём в кино́ сего́дня ве́чером. (We're going to go to the movies tonight.)

По- with indeterminate verbs indicates an action that goes on "for a while":

Де́ти побе́гали в саду́ и верну́лись домо́й. (The children ran around in the garden for a while and returned home.)

Unlike most other prefixed verbs formed from indeterminate verbs, these are perfective.

Many of the prefixed verbs above are very close in meaning and consequently may be difficult to distinguish. In particular, уйти́ and пойти́ may present problems. The two verbs are almost identical in meaning, but there are some differences in the way they are used. Уйти́ can be used without a reference to the destination: Они́ ушли́. (They left.) Пойти́ cannot: Они́ пошли́ в банк. (They went to the bank.)

In sentences with уйти́, both the place a person is leaving and the place to which a person is going can be stated (although both rarely are mentioned in the same sentence):

Они́ ушли́ из магази́на. Они́ ушли́ в шко́лу.
(They left the store. They left for school.)

In sentences with пойти́, only the destination is stated:

Они́ пошли́ в шко́лу. (They went to school.)

Idiomatic Use of Verbs of Motion

Note that in the unprefixed verbs below, generally only one form (determinate or indeterminate) is acceptable in the idiomatic use of these verbs. You cannot, for example, say нести пальто and mean it figuratively. It is, however, quite acceptable in the literal meaning. This list, of course, provides just a sample of idiomatic uses for verbs of motion.

время идёт	time passes
время проходит	time passes
годы идут	time passes
время бежит	time flies
время летит	time flies
дождь идёт	it is raining
снег идёт	it is snowing
урок идёт	the lesson is going on
вести урок	to conduct a class
вести переговоры	to conduct negotiations
вести разговор	to conduct a conversation
вести себя	to behave oneself
носить очки	to wear glasses
носить пальто	to wear a coat
платье идёт	the dress is becoming
выводить/вывести (кого-нибудь) из терпения	to make (someone) lose patience
сойти с ума	to lose one's mind
провести/проводить лето	to spend the summer
провести/проводить время	to spend time

§12.12 VERBS OF POSITION

Russian verbs of position and verbs of getting into position can be broken down into the following categories:

1. Getting into position

Imperfective	Perfective	
ложиться	лечь	to lie down
садиться	сесть	to sit down
вставать	встать	to stand up

2. Being in position

Imperfective	Perfective	
лежа́ть	полежа́ть	to be lying
сиде́ть	посиде́ть	to be sitting
стоя́ть	постоя́ть	to be standing
висе́ть	повисе́ть	to hang

3. Placing someone or something into position

Imperfective	Perfective	
класть	положи́ть	to lay (someone or something) down
сажа́ть	посади́ть	to sit (someone or something) down
ста́вить	поста́вить	to stand (someone or something) up
ве́шать	пове́сить	to hang (someone or something) up

Be careful to choose the right verb—each of these verbs has a specific meaning and cannot be replaced by another.

The first group of verbs describes actions that apply to people or animals:

Мы се́ли за стол. (We sat down to the table.)

Ка́ждый день, он встаёт в семь часо́в. (Every day he gets up at seven o'clock.)

Ири́на ля́жет спать когда́ прочита́ет кни́гу. (Irina will go to bed when she finishes reading the book.)

The second group of verbs consists of actions that can apply to people, animals, or things. Unlike the verbs in the other two categories, these verbs describe people, animals, or objects in a stationary position.

Почему́ журна́лы лежа́т на полу́? (Why are the magazines lying on the floor?)

Почему́ ты лежи́шь на полу́? (Why are you lying on the floor?)

Ва́за стоя́ла на по́лке, а тепе́рь она́ стои́т на столе́. (The vase was standing on the shelf, and now it's on the table.)

Я здесь посижу́ пять мину́т. (I'll sit here for five minutes.)

Карти́на виси́т на стене́. (The painting is hanging on the wall.)

The third group of verbs describes actions that are performed by people upon other people, animals, or things. In other words, a person may stand someone or something up, lay someone or something down, hang something up, or sit someone down. On rare occasions, one may sit some-*thing* down—a doll, for instance. (Be careful with вѐшать/повѐсить: when it is used in reference to some*one*, it means execution by hanging.)

> Вѐся поставил стакан воды на стол. (Vasya put a glass of water on the table.)
> Мы посадим ребёнка в коляску. (We'll sit the baby down in the stroller.)
> Надо повесить пальто в шкаф. ([You] should hang the coat in the closet.)
> Она всегда кладёт газеты под стол. (She always puts the newspapers under the table.)

Класть/положить also serves as the general-purpose verb of placement. In the sentence Ребёнок кладёт игрушки в шкаф (The child is putting the toys into the cupboard), it may be hard to say whether the toys are placed in a standing position or laid down flat. It is most likely that they are all jumbled up. But it does not matter—in cases such as this, класть/положить has the general meaning "to put, place."

Сажать/посадить has another, more frequently used, meaning in addition to the one given above: to plant (trees, flowers, seeds, etc.).

Сажать and сидеть have another specialized and figurative meaning in addition to their general meaning:

> Его посадили в тюрьму. (He was put in prison.)
> Он много лет сидел в тюрьме. (He spent many years in prison.)

Сидеть (but not сажать) can also be used in the following context:

> Она сегодня сидит дома. (She's at home today.)

Лежать and положить also have a specialized and figurative meaning in addition to their general meaning:

> Его положили в больницу. (He was put in the hospital.)
> Он лежит в больнице. (He's in the hospital.)

The verbs of position given in the chart above can be used in sequence to describe an entire series of actions:

> Дедушка садится на диван. Он сидит на диване. Он встаёт с дивана. Он стоит. (Grandfather sits down on the couch. He's sitting on the couch. He gets up from the couch. He's standing.)

Ка́тя положи́ла кни́гу на стол. Кни́га лежа́ла на столе́. Ли́за поста́вила кни́гу на по́лку. Тепе́рь кни́га стои́т на по́лке. (Katya laid the book on the table. The book lay on the table. Liza stood the book on the shelf. The book is now standing on the shelf.)

The verb pair станови́ться/стать (to stand, get into a standing position) also belongs in the category of verbs of position:

Она́ ста́ла у двери́. (She went and stood by the door.)

Far more frequently, however, it is used in its other meaning, "to become or to begin."

As mentioned in an earlier section, some of these verbs take -ся while the corresponding verb in the verb pair does not. Note, however, that most of these verbs do not take -ся. Ве́шать/пове́сить may do so, but the addition of -ся changes the meaning considerably, because ве́шаться/пове́ситься means "to hang oneself." If you use it in reference to a painting, for example, it will mean that the painting hung itself on the wall.

§12.13 PARTICIPLES

Participles are words that have characteristics of verbs and of adjectives. Like verbs, participles have tense and aspect. Like adjectives, they agree with nouns and take adjectival endings.

You will encounter participles most often in written Russian. They are not common in spoken Russian.

Participles may be active or passive. An active participle is one that applies to the actor who performs the action expressed by the participle:

Челове́к, пи́шущий на доске́, профе́ссор. (The person who is writing on the board is the professor.)

Пи́шущий, the participle, applies to челове́к, who performs the action of the participle (writing). A passive participle is one that applies to the object of the action of the participle:

Письмо́, напи́санное им, лежи́т на столе́. (The letter written by him is lying on the table.)

Напи́санное, the participle, applies to письмо́, the object of the action of the participle (writing).

Formation of Present Active Participles
To form a present active participle, add one of the following suffixes to the nonpast stem of a verb (for the formation of the nonpast stem, see the beginning of §12.5-2):

First Conjugation Verbs	-ущ- / -ющ-
Second Conjugation Verbs	-ащ- / -ящ-

Note that hard vowel variants and soft vowel variants appear above. Use whichever variant is needed for a particular verb. The vowel will be identical to the vowel in the third person plural ending of the verb.

After you add the suffix to the nonpast stem, you must add endings. The endings are the same as those used for long-form descriptive adjectives (see §10.5-1), and the same rules of agreement apply as for adjectives. In the sentences above, for example, пишущий has a nominative masculine singular adjectival ending because человéк, the word to which it refers, is a masculine singular noun in the nominative. When adding adjectival endings, keep in mind that, as always, the spelling rules apply.

Only imperfective verbs form present active participles.

The chart below summarizes the steps that must be taken to form present active participles:

Infinitive	Nonpast Stem	Suffix	Nominative Ending	Example of Present Active Participle
говорúть (to speak)	говор-	-ящ-	-ий, -ее, -ая, -ие	говорящий
читáть (to read)	чита (j)-	-ющ-	-ий, -ее, -ая, -ие	читáющая
писáть (to write)	пиш-	-ущ-	-ий, -ее, -ая, -ие	пишущее
лежáть (to lie down)	леж-	-ащ-	-ий, -ее, -ая, -ие	лежáщий

Formation of Past Active Participles
To form a past active participle, add one of the following suffixes to the past stem of a verb (for the formation of the past stem, see the beginning of §12.5-1):

if the past stem ends in a vowel, add: вш-
if the past stem ends in a consonant, add: -ш-

Exceptions: идтú (to walk)—шéдший (-ее, -ая, -ие)
вестú (to lead)—вéдший (-ее, -ая, -ие)

After you add the suffix to the past stem, add the adjectival endings used for long-form descriptive adjectives (see §10.5-1). The ending must agree with the noun to which the participle refers. The spelling rules apply, as always.

Both perfective and imperfective verbs can be used to form past active participles.

The chart below summarizes the steps that must be taken to form past active participles:

Infinitive	Past Stem	Suffix	Nominative Ending	Example of Past Active Participle
говори́ть (to speak)	говори-	-вш-	-ий, -ее, -ая, -ие	говори́вшая
чита́ть (to read)	чита-	-вш-	-ий, -ee, -ая, -ие	чита́вший
писа́ть (to write)	писа-	-вш-	-ий, -ee, -ая, -ие	писа́вшие
нести́ (to carry)	нес-	-ш-	-ий, -ee, -ая, -ие	нёсшая

Formation of Present Passive Participles

To form a present passive participle, add one of the following suffixes to the nonpast stem of a verb (for the formation of the nonpast stem, see the beginning of §12.5-2):

First Conjugation Verbs   -ем-
Second Conjugation Verbs   -им-

Note that the form will be identical to the first person plural of the verb. After you add the suffix to the nonpast stem, add the adjectival endings that are used for long-form descriptive adjectives (see §10.5-1). The ending must agree with the noun to which the participle refers.

Only imperfective verbs form present passive participles. Intransitive verbs and verbs ending in -ся cannot form present passive participles.

The chart below summarizes the steps that must be taken to form present passive participles:

Infinitive	Nonpast Stem	Suffix	Nomi- native Ending	Example of Present Passive Participle
решáть (to try to solve, decide)	реша-	-ем-	-ый, -ое, -ая, -ые	решáемая
вѝдеть (to see)	вид-	-им-	-ый, -ое, -ая, -ые	вѝдимый

Several verbs have irregular present passive participles. Verbs ending in -давать, -ставать, and -знавать do not lose -ва- in the formation of the present passive participle:

узнавáть (to try to find out, recognize)—узнавáемый
отдавáть (to give away)—отдавáемый

In general, the present passive participle does not occur frequently and is limited to formal use. Many verbs do not even have present passive forms. If you are unsure whether a verb has a present passive participle form, check in a book such as Patricia Davis's *201 Russian Verbs* (Barron's) to see if a form is listed.

Formation of Past Passive Participles
To form a past passive participle, add one of the following suffixes to the past stem of a verb (for the formation of the past stem, see the beginning of §12.5-1):

Verbs ending in ать, -еть, and -ять	-нн-
Verbs ending in -ить and -ти	-енн-
Verbs ending in -нуть and -ыть	-т-

Verbs ending in -ить undergo consonant mutation when the past passive participle is formed: замéтить (to notice)— замéченный. See the appendix for a chart on consonant mutation.

Some verbs have irregular past passive participles. Although they end in -ать and -ять, взять, начáть, and verbs that end in -нять take -т- as a suffix (instead of the expected -нн-):

взять (to take)—взятый
начáть (to begin)—нáчатый
занять (to occupy)—зáнятый

Monosyllabic verbs that end in -еть or -ить and their prefixed forms also take -т-:

прожи́ть (to live)—прожи́тый
вы́лить (to pour out)—вы́литый
спеть (to sing)—спе́тый

The past passive participle of вести́ (to lead, take along [when walking]) and its prefixed forms require the nonpast stem: переведённый.

Verbs that end in -ереть take -т- in the past passive participle. They lose the last -e- before the addition of the suffix:

запере́ть (to lock)—за́пертый

As with other participles, you must add adjectival endings after the suffix of past passive participles. The endings are those used for long-form descriptive adjectives (see §10.5-1). The same rules of agreement apply as for adjectives in general.

Only perfective transitive verbs can be used to form past passive participles. The past passive participle is encountered fairly frequently in Russian.

The chart below summarizes the steps that must be taken to form past passive participles:

Infinitive	Nonpast Stem	Suffix	Nominative Ending	Example of Past Passive Participle
прочита́ть (to read)	прочита-	-нн-	-ый, -ое, -ая, -ые	прочи́танное
бро́сить (to throw)	броси- брош-	-енн-	-ый, -ое, -ая, -ые	бро́шенный
дости́гнуть (to achieve)	достигну-	-т-	-ый, -ое, -ая, -ые	дости́гнутые

Stress may present a problem in past passive participles. If the stress in the past tense of a verb falls before the suffix of the past tense form, then it will remain on the same syllable in the past passive participle. If it falls on the suffix, however, in most cases it will move back to the stem in the past passive participle. If an infinitive ends in -ать or -нуть, the stress will always move back: написа́ть (to write)—напи́санный.

If an infinitive ends in -ить, the stress may or may not move back: изучи́ть (to study)—изу́ченный, but освети́ть (to light, enlighten)—освещённый. The rule of thumb for -ить verbs is that the stress is the same as it is in the third person plural form.

The Use of Participles

Participles occur in the same kinds of situations as кото́рый clauses. Past active participles and present active participles are used when кото́рый is the subject of the clause:

> Мы ви́дели профе́ссора, кото́рый живёт на на́шей у́лице. Мы ви́дели профе́ссора, живу́щего на на́шей у́лице. (We saw the professor who lives on our street.)
> Же́нщина, кото́рая написа́ла э́тот интере́сный рома́н, рабо́тала в на́шей библиоте́ке. Же́нщина, написа́вшая э́тот интере́сный рома́н, рабо́тала в на́шей библиоте́ке. (The woman who wrote that interesting novel worked in our library.)

As you can see, кото́рый is removed and the verb in the same clause is turned into a participle. It takes the same tense and aspect as the verb: for example, if the verb is a perfective in the past tense, the perfective past active participle is used. The participle agrees in gender, number, and case with the noun in the other clause to which it refers: профе́ссора (masculine, singular, accusative)—живу́щего (masculine, singular, accusative).

Everything else in the two sentences is the same. Note that all the sentences above contain two clauses. The second set contains a clause that is split up. же́нщина . . . рабо́тала в на́шей библиоте́ке. In both types of sentences, however, the participle immediately follows the noun to which it refers: . . . же́нщина, написа́вшая . . .

Two clauses, however, are not always required:

> В библиоте́ке мы ви́дели студе́нтов, кото́рые занима́ются. В библиоте́ке мы ви́дели занима́ющихся студе́нтов. (In the library, we saw students who were studying.)

Here the participle is placed in front of the noun to which it refers. (Note that verbs ending in -ся also have participles. Form the participle in the regular way, then add -ся to the end. The variant -сь is not used with participles.)

Past passive participles and present passive participles are used in sentences where кото́рый is the accusative object of the clause and is not preceded by a preposition:

> Ле́кция, кото́рую чита́ет профе́ссор, интере́сная. (The lecture that the professor is delivering is interesting.)
> Ле́кция, чита́емая профе́ссором, интере́сная. (The lecture being delivered by the professor is interesting.)

Газе́ты, кото́рые они́ принесли́, лежа́т на по́лке. (The newspapers that they brought are lying on the shelf.)
Газе́ты, принесённые и́ми, лежа́т на по́лке. (The newspapers brought by them are lying on the shelf.)

Note the following:

1. The subject of the clause containing the passive participle must be put into the instrumental case.

2. The suffix -енн-, when stressed, becomes -ённ-.

In addition, the same changes occur as for active participles: кото́рый is removed; the verb is replaced with a participle of the same tense and aspect; and the participle agrees in gender, number, and case with the noun in the other clause to which it refers.

As in the case of sentences with active participles, these sentences may contain two clauses, one of which may be split. In all these sentences, the participle immediately follows the noun to which it refers: Газе́ты, принесённые . . .

These sentences also may contain only one clause:

Пришло́ письмо́, кото́рое он написа́л. (The letter that he wrote arrived.)
Пришло́ напи́санное им письмо́. (The letter written by him arrived.)

Both the participle and the noun of the original second clause are moved in front of the noun to which the participle refers.

Sentences containing participles are generally rather rare and are considered bookish. Sentences containing кото́рый occur much more frequently. This is especially true in spoken Russian.

Short-Form Passive Participles

The passive participles given above are long forms. They take the endings that are used for long-form descriptive adjectives. Short-form passive participles are formed in the same way as long-form passive participles, but they take different endings. They require the same endings as those used for short-form descriptive adjectives:

Masculine	Neuter	Feminine	Plural
—	-о	-а	-ы

	Infinitive	Long Form	Short Form
Compare:	решáть (to try to decide, solve)	решáемая	решáема
	взять (to take)	взятые	взяты

Participles with suffixes containing -нн- lose one н in the short form: прочи́танная—прочи́тана.

Short-form passive participles agree in gender and number with the nouns to which they refer. They do not change for case.

Unlike long-form passive participles, short-form passive participles are used predicatively. In other words, they are connected to the subject through a verb:

Окнó бы́ло закры́то. (The window was closed).

The verb will indicate the tense. Short-form passive participles have no tense themselves.

Sentences with short-form passive participles cannot be used to replace sentences with котóрый. The short forms may, however, be used in котóрый clauses:

Мяч, котóрый был брóшен под стол, принадлежи́т э́тому ма́ленькому ма́льчику. (The ball, which was thrown under the table, belongs to that little boy.)

When removing котóрый in such a sentence, you must also remove the auxiliary verb (in this case, был) and convert the short form into a long-form past passive participle.

Short forms of present passive participles are rare, but those formed from past passive participles are fairly common.

Some stress shifts occur in short-form passive participles. If the stress falls on -ен- (making it -ён-) in the masculine singular, it moves to the ending in all other forms. If a stress shift occurs in the past tense forms of a verb, it will also affect the short-form passive participle.

§12.14 VERBAL ADVERBS (GERUNDS)

Verbal adverbs (also known as gerunds) are words that have characteristics of verbs and of adverbs. Like verbs, they have tense and aspect. Like adverbs, they modify actions and they do not change for gender, number, or case.

The Formation of Verbal Adverbs

The Formation of Verbal Adverbs from Imperfective Verbs
Verbal adverbs from imperfective verbs are formed by adding -я to the nonpast stem (for the formation of the nonpast stem, see the beginning of §12.5-2). After ж, ч, ш, and щ, because of the spelling rules, а is written instead of я. For verbs ending in -ся, the verbal adverb ends in -ясь/-ась.

Infinitive	Nonpast Stem	Suffix	Imperfective Verbal Adverb
сидеть (to sit)	сид-	-я	сидя
разговаривать (to converse)	разговарива-	-я	разговаривая
слышать (to hear)	слыш-	-а	слыша
заниматься (to study, to be occupied)	занима-	-ясь	занимаясь

Exceptions
Verbs ending in -давать, -знавать, and -ставать do not lose -ва- in the formation of the verbal adverb:

подавать (to give)—подавая
вставать (to get up)—вставая

The verbal adverb form of быть (to be) is будучи, but it is rarely encountered.

Some verbs do not have verbal adverbs or do not have verbal adverbs that are used. Among these verbs are those with infinitives ending in -чь and -нуть as well as:

писать (to write)
бежать (to run)
петь (to sing)
пить (to drink)

лить (to pour)
бить (to hit, strike)
шить (to sew)
ждать (to wait)—use ожидая, from ожидáть (to wait)
хотéть (to want)—use желáя, from желáть (to wish, desire)
смотрéть (to look, watch)—use глядя, from глядéть (to look [at])

The Formation of Verbal Adverbs from Perfective Verbs

Verbal adverbs from perfective verbs are formed by adding the suffix -в to the past stem of verbs that end in vowels (for the formation of the past stem, see the beginning of §12.5-1). The variant -вши is also possible (one can say открыв or открывши, for example) but it is encountered less frequently. The suffix -вши must be used, however, with verbs ending in -ся, and -ся will take the form -сь.

Infinitive	Past Stem	Suffix	Perfective Verbal Adverb
прочитáть (to read)	прочита-	-в	прочитáв
посмотрéть (to look, watch)	посмотре-	-в	посмотрéв
закрыться (to close)	закры- (-ся)	-вши	закрывшись

Exceptions

Prefixed forms of идти (to walk), нести (to carry), вести (to lead), and везти (to transport [by vehicle]) take the suffix -я, the same one that is used for verbal adverbs formed from imperfective verbs. This suffix is added to the nonpast stem. Only the prefixes, which make the verbs perfective, distinguish these verbal adverbs from their counterparts formed from imperfective verbs:

принести (to bring)—принеся
пойти (to go [on foot])—пойдя

The Use of Verbal Adverbs

Imperfective verbal adverbs are used when the action of the verbal adverb and the action of the verb are simultaneous:

Стóя в óчереди, мы разговáривали. (Standing in line, we talked. [We talked while standing in line.])

The tense of the verb can change, but the form of the imperfective verbal adverb will not change:

Стоя в очереди, мы разговариваем. (Standing in line, we talk. [We are talking while standing in line.])

Стоя в очереди, мы будем разговаривать. (Standing in line, we will talk. [We will talk while standing in line.])

In sentences that contain verbal adverbs, the verb describes the main action of the sentence, while the verbal adverb provides the background action. A similar sentence could consist of two verbs:

Мы стоим в очереди и разговариваем. (We are standing in line and talking.)

Such use of two verbs would indicate that both actions are seen as having equal importance. Note that because the actions are simultaneous, imperfective verbs are used.

In contrast to imperfective verbal adverbs, perfective verbal adverbs are used when the action of the verbal adverb precedes the action of the verb:

Открыв дверь, он увидел Васю. (Having opened the door, he saw Vasya. [After opening the door, he saw Vasya.])

As in the constructions with imperfective verbal adverbs, the tense of the verb can change in such sentences. The form of the verbal adverb will remain the same.

The verb describes the main action of the sentence, while the verbal adverb provides the background action. A similar sentence could contain two verbs, in which case both actions would be seen as equally important. Because the actions described are mentioned in sequence, the two verbs would have to be perfective:

Он открыл дверь и увидел Васю. (He opened the door and saw Vasya.)

As you can see from the examples of the imperfective verbal adverbs and the perfective verbal adverbs above, the tense of verbal adverbs depends on the tense of the main verb. Verbal adverbs themselves do not have tense.

Verbal adverbs must always refer to the subject of the sentence. You cannot say, for example, Идя в магазин, пошёл дождь (Going to the store, the rain started), because the subject is дождь (rain) and идя (going) refers to the person who is walking to the store.

Constructions with verbal adverbs are set off by commas.

Sentences containing verbal adverbs generally can be replaced by sentences with когда (when) clauses:

Стоя в очереди, мы разговаривали. (Standing in line, we talked. [We
   talked while standing in line.])
Когда мы стояли в очереди, мы разговаривали. (When we were
   standing in line we were talking.)

Открыв дверь, он увидел Васю. (Having opened the door, he saw
   Vasya. [After opening the door, he saw Vasya.])
Когда он открыл дверь, он увидел Васю. (When he opened the door,
   he saw Vasya.)

Note, however, that although когда is used in both sentences, it does not change the temporal relationships: in the
first sentence, the two actions are simultaneous; in the second, the first action precedes the second.

§12.15 PASSIVE VOICE

Active sentences can be turned into passive ones by taking
several steps. Compare the two sentences below, for
example:

Соня прочитала газету. (Sonia read the paper.) [active]
Газета была прочитана Соней. (The paper was read by Sonia.)
   [passive]

The accusative direct object in the active sentence
becomes the nominative subject of the passive sentence.
The original nominative subject, Соня, is expressed in the
instrumental. The verb is turned into a passive participle —
in this case, a short-form past passive participle. An auxiliary verb is also added.

§13.

Adverbs

Adverbs are words that modify verbs, adjectives, or other adverbs. They describe manner, intensity, quantity, place, or time.

Adverbs do not change for gender, number, or case. They are invariable—they take only one form. There are different types of adverbs, however, that must be learned. They are given and discussed in §13.4.

Adverbs generally precede the words they modify, but if an adverb is placed at the end of a sentence, it tends to carry more emphasis. Adverbs can sometimes appear at the beginning of a sentence (for example, interrogative adverbs).

Adverbs of Manner

Adverbs of manner answer the question как? (how?):

Са́ша **пло́хо** пи́шет. (Sasha writes badly.)
Де́ти **хорошо́** игра́ют вме́сте. (The children play well together.)
Нам бы́ло **интере́сно** слу́шать докла́д. (We found it interesting to listen to the lecture.)
Ле́на бу́дет чита́ть **вслух**. (Lena is going to read aloud.)
Мы говори́м **по-ру́сски**. (We speak Russian.)

Note the similarity in form between some adverbs and adjectives (for example, интере́сно—интере́сный [interesting]). But adverbs, as stated above, modify verbs, adjectives, or other adverbs, while adjectives modify nouns. Compare:

Он всегда́ говори́т **ти́хо**. [adverb] (He always speaks quietly.)
Он всегда́ был **ти́хим** челове́ком. [adjective] (He was always a quiet person.)
Они́ прие́хали **бы́стро**. [adverb] (They arrived quickly.)
Они́ прие́хали на **бы́стром** по́езде. [adjective] (They arrived on a fast train.)

This distinction is especially important when using short-form neuter singular adjectives, which have the same form as some adverbs. Compare:

Она́ **споко́йно** рабо́тает. [adverb] (She works calmly.)
Мо́ре сейча́с **споко́йно**. [adjective] (The sea is now calm.)

Adverbs of Place

Adverbs of place answer the questions где? (where?), куда? (where to?), or откуда? (from where?):

> Мы пошли **домой**. (We went home.)
> Он стоит **впереди**. (He's standing in front.)
> Нам надо повернуть **направо**. (We need to turn right.)

The adverb of place that you choose will depend on the question (куда? где? откуда?) that you are answering:

куда? **(where to?)**	где? **(where?)**	откуда? **(from where?)**
домой (home)	дома (at home)	
назад (backwards)	сзади (behind)	
вперёд (forward)	впереди (in front)	
направо (to the right)	направо (on the right)	
налево (to the left)	налево (on the left)	
внутрь (inside)	внутри (Inside)	изнутри (from inside)
наружу (outside)	снаружи (outside)	снаружи (from outside)
вниз (down, downstairs)	внизу (below, downstairs)	снизу (from below)
наверх (up, upstairs); вверх (up)	наверху (above, upstairs)	сверху (from above)
——	везде (everywhere)	отовсюду (from everywhere)

(To indicate leaving the house, use из дому. Note that the stress is marked on the preposition—pronounce the two words as one, with the stress on the first syllable.) Compare the following sentences:

> Он нас ждёт **внизу**. (He's waiting for us downstairs.)
> Мы сейчас пойдём **вниз**. (We're going downstairs now.)
> Мы на балконе. Он нас видит **снизу**. (We're on a balcony. He sees us from below.)

One final note: наверх (up, upstairs) is generally used when referring to enclosed spaces; вверх (up), on the other hand, can be used in reference to open or closed spaces.

> Она пошла **наверх**. (She went upstairs.)
> Самолёт полетел **вверх**. (The plane flew up.)

Adverbs of Time

Adverbs of time answer the questions когда? (when?), сколько времени? (how long?), or как часто? (how frequently?):

Мы вас **долго** ждали. (We waited for you for a long time.)
Коля приехал **весной**. (Kolya arrived in the spring.)
Он **часто** должен ходить к врачу. (He has to go to the doctor often.)

Some commonly used adverbs of time

вчера	yesterday
сегодня	today
завтра	tomorrow
позавчера	the day before yesterday
послезавтра	the day after tomorrow
утром	in the morning
днём	in the daytime
вечером	in the evening
ночью	at night
весной	in the spring
летом	in the summer
осенью	in the fall
зимой	in the winter
теперь	now, at present
сейчас	now, very soon
сразу	right away
давно	a long time ago, for a long time
недавно	not long ago, recently
раньше	earlier, before, formerly
однажды	once, one day
сначала	at first, at the beginning, from the beginning
потом	after, later
рано	early
поздно	late
вовремя	in time
скоро	soon
всегда	always
обычно	usually
иногда	sometimes
никогда	never
долго	(for) a long time
недолго	(for) a short time
часто	frequently
редко	rarely

Adverbs of Measure or Degree

Adverbs of measure or degree answer the questions сколько? (how much? how many?) or до какой степени? (to what degree?):

Вы **много** читаете? (Do you read a great deal?)
Он **совсем** не понял меня. (He completely misunderstood me.)
Снег **почти** исчез. (The snow has almost disappeared.)

Some commonly used adverbs of measure or degree

мно́го	much, a great deal, a lot
ма́ло	little (not in reference to size)
немно́го	not much, some
о́чень	very
совсе́м	completely, quite, entirely
сли́шком	too
доста́точно	enough
почти́	almost, nearly
вдво́е	twice as much
втро́е	three times as much
два́жды	twice
три́жды	three times

As stated earlier, adverbs modify not only verbs, but also adjectives and adverbs. Adverbs of measure and degree provide good examples of adverbial use with adjectives and adverbs:

Она́ **о́чень хорошо́** написа́ла рабо́ту. [an adverb modifies an adverb]
(She wrote the paper very well.)
Э́тот костю́м **сли́шком большо́й**. [an adverb modifies an adjective]
(This suit is too big.)

Other Adverbs

The demonstrative, interrogative, relative, indefinite, and negative adverbs that follow do not describe or modify anything; instead, they only make reference to place, time, manner, measure, or degree. These adverbs have the same forms as pronouns.

Demonstrative Adverbs
Some commonly used demonstrative adverbs

здесь	here (in reference to location)
тут	here (in reference to location)
там	there (in reference to location)
сюда́	here (in reference to motion toward someone or something)
туда́	there (in reference to motion toward someone or something)
отсю́да	from here (in reference to motion away from someone or something)
отту́да	from there (in reference to motion away from someone or something)
так	so
тогда́	then
сто́лько	so much, so many
потому́	that is why

Он е́здил **туда́**. (He went there.)
Купи́ **сто́лько**, ско́лько ну́жно. (Buy as much as is needed.)

Interrogative and Relative Adverbs
Some commonly used interrogative and relative adverbs

где	where (in reference to location)
куда́	where (in reference to motion toward someone or something)
отку́да	from where (in reference to motion away from someone or something)
как	how
когда́	when
ско́лько	how much, how many
почему́	why

Отку́да они́ пришли́? (Where did they come from?)
Я забы́ла, **ско́лько** сто́ит э́та блу́зка. (I forgot how much this blouse costs.)

Indefinite Adverbs
Some commonly used indefinite adverbs

где́-то	somewhere (in reference to location)
где́-нибудь	somewhere (in reference to location)
куда́-то	somewhere (in reference to motion toward someone or something)
куда́-нибудь	somewhere (in reference to motion toward someone or something)
отку́да-то	from somewhere (in reference to motion away from someone or something)
отку́да-нибудь	from somewhere (in reference to motion away from someone or something)
ка́к-то	somehow
ка́к-нибудь	somehow
когда́-то	once (upon a time), at one time
когда́-нибудь	sometime
почему́-то	for some reason

Мари́на и Пе́тя **куда́-то** уе́хали. (Marina and Petya went somewhere.)
Я **когда́-нибудь** позвоню́. (I'll call sometime.)

Note that these adverbs resemble interrogative adverbs, with the addition of the particles -то or -нибудь. For a discussion of the differences between -то and -нибудь, and the way to determine which one to use, see §11.7.

Negative Adverbs
Some commonly used negative adverbs

нигде́	nowhere (in reference to location)
никуда́	nowhere (in reference to motion toward someone or something)
ниотку́да	from nowhere (in reference to motion away from someone or something)
ника́к	in no way
никогда́	never

Они́ **никогда́** не хо́дят в теа́тр. (They never go to the theater.)
То́ля **нигде́** не был сего́дня. (Tolya didn't go anywhere today.)

These adverbs are similar to interrogative adverbs, with the addition of the particle ни-. Note that the negative particle не must also be used with negative adverbs. It is placed immediately before the verb.

Comparative Adverbs

Comparative adverbs exist only for qualitative adverbs, that is, those which describe qualities. Comparative adverbs are formed in the same ways as comparative adjectives. A comparative adverb can be formed by placing бóлее (more) or мéнее (less) in front of an adverb.

Compare:

> Онá говорит **бóлее интерéсно**, чем он. [adverb] (She speaks in a more interesting way than he does.)
> У неё был **бóлее интерéсный** доклáд, чем у негó. [adjective] (She gave a more interesting lecture than he did.)

Like comparative adjectives, comparative adverbs can also be formed by using -ee. Comparative adverbs of this type are identical to the simple comparative form of adjectives. To form comparative adverbs, follow the rules on the formation of simple comparative adjectives in §10.5-5. The same exceptions apply as well.

Compare:

> Юра **быстрéе** Андрéя. [adjective] (Yura is faster than Andrei.)
> Юра бежит **быстрéе** Андрéя. [adverb] (Yura runs faster than Andrei.)

Keep in mind that, although the forms are identical, the functions of comparative adjectives and adverbs are different. The adjectives modify nouns, the adverbs modify verbs.

Superlative Adverbs

Superlative adverbs are formed by adding всех (the genitive plural form of все [all]) to the comparative form of the adverb:

> Юра бежит быстрéе всех. (Yura runs faster than everybody.)

Impersonal Constructions with Adverbs

Some impersonal constructions require the use of adverbs. Because they also require the dative case, they are discussed in the section on the dative. See "Impersonal constructions with adverbs" in §9.3-5 for a discussion of this subject.

§14.

Numbers

1 один (masc.) одно́ (neut.) одна́ (fem.) одни́ (plur.)	20 два́дцать
	30 три́дцать
2 два (masc. and neut.) две (fem.)	40 со́рок
3 три	50 пятьдеся́т
4 четы́ре	60 шестьдеся́т
5 пять	70 се́мьдесят
6 шесть	80 во́семьдесят
7 семь	90 девяно́сто
8 во́семь	100 сто
9 де́вять	200 две́сти
10 де́сять	300 три́ста
11 оди́ннадцать	400 четы́реста
12 двена́дцать	500 пятьсо́т
13 трина́дцать	600 шестьсо́т
14 четы́рнадцать	700 семьсо́т
15 пятна́дцать	800 восемьсо́т
16 шестна́дцать	900 девятьсо́т
17 семна́дцать	1,000 ты́сяча
18 восемна́дцать	1,000,000 миллио́н
19 девятна́дцать	1,000,000,000 миллиа́рд

In Russian, the number "one" changes for gender—it agrees with the noun which it qualifies. Oddly enough, it also has a plural form, which is used with nouns that exist only in the plural (see §9.3-1):

У меня́ то́лько одни́ часы́. (I have only one watch.)

Оди́н, одно́, одна́, and одни́ also have figurative uses. They are:

1. alone

Он оста́лся оди́н. (He remained alone.)

2. the same

Все пи́ли из одно́й ча́шки. (Everyone drank from the same cup.)

3. a certain

Оди́н студе́нт сказа́л, что он не хо́чет занима́ться. (A certain student said that he doesn't want to study.)

4. some

Одни́ лю́ди голосова́ли за президе́нта, други́е голосова́ли про́тив. (Some people voted for the president, others voted against.)

5. only; nothing but

Она́ одна́ зна́ет, где докуме́нты. (Only she knows where the documents are.)
Алёша пьёт одну́ во́ду. (Alyosha drinks nothing but water.)

The number "two" has two forms in Russian. Два is for masculine and neuter nouns, and две is for feminine nouns. Note one unusual characteristic: the form that ends in -a is not the feminine form.

After 2, numbers do not change for gender (три, четы́ре, пять [3, 4, 5]), but compounds that include 1 and 2 do change for gender: сто оди́н, сто одна́ (101), два́дцать два, два́дцать две (22).

The spelling of numbers presents some problems. The numbers 11 through 20 and the number 30 have a soft sign only at the end: for example, восемна́дцать (18).

The numbers 50, 60, 70, and 80 and the numbers 500, 600, 700, 800, and 900 have a soft sign after the first part of the compound number, but no soft sign at the end: for example, се́мьдесят (70).

The numbers between 10 and 20 are written as one word, but the numbers between 20 and 30, 30 and 40, and up are written as two: for example, девяно́сто шесть (96).

As mentioned in §9.3-3, the genitive case must follow cardinal numbers except 1 and its compounds (21, 31, etc., but not 11). Treat 1 and its compounds as you would any other adjectives. As for the other numbers: sometimes the genitive singular follows them, sometimes the genitive plural.

Numbers:	Case and Number of the Adjective That Follows:	Case and Number of the Noun That Follows:
2, 3, 4, or their compounds	genitive plural (for feminines— nominative plural also possible)	genitive singular
5–10 or their compounds, and 11–14	genitive plural	genitive plural

Note:

1. After 2, 3, 4, and their compounds, a nominative plural adjective may be used before a feminine noun:

Две большие машины стоят в гараже. (Two big cars are parked in the garage.)

2. Substantivized adjectives should be treated like any other adjectives:

Эти два учёных (gen. plur.) работают в институте. (These two scholars work at the institute.)

Keep in mind that the rules in this chart apply only when the noun affected by the numbers is in the nominative or accusative position in the sentence.

Я ему дала шесть **старых книг**. (I gave him six old books.)
Тридцать два **опытных врача** работают в этой больнице.
(Thirty-two experienced doctors work in this hospital.)

In cases other than the nominative or accusative, numbers behave differently: like adjectives, they agree with the noun to which they refer and do not require that the noun be in the genitive. In other words, the noun affects the case of the number, not vice versa.

Numbers are declined; unfortunately, they are not all declined in the same way.

The number "one" has a declension similar to этот (this, that) and, as stated above, is treated as an adjective in all cases.

	Masculine	**Neuter**	**Feminine**	**Plural**
Nom.	один	одно́	одна́	одни́
Acc.	like nom. or gen.	одно́	одну́	like nom. or gen.
Gen.	одного́		одно́й	одни́х
Prep.	одно́м		одно́й	одни́х
Dat.	одному́		одно́й	одни́м
Inst.	одни́м		одно́й	одни́ми

Example: Они́ все прие́хали на одно́й маши́не. (They all arrived in one car.)

(The masculine and plural accusative will be like the genitive when the noun is animate, and like the nominative when the noun is inanimate.)

The numbers 2, 3, and 4 belong to a second category:

Nom.	два	две	три	четы́ре
Acc.	like nom. or gen.		like nom. or gen.	like nom. or gen.
Gen.	двух		трёх	четырёх
Prep.	двух		трёх	четырёх
Dat.	двум		трём	четырём
Inst.	двумя́		тремя́	четырьмя́

Example: Учи́тель говори́т с тремя́ ученика́ми. (The teacher is speaking with three students.)

(The accusative will be like the genitive when the noun is animate, and like the nominative when the noun is inanimate. The distinction between animate and inanimate in the accusative case does not apply to compounds ending in 2, 3, and 4, but only to 2, 3, and 4.)

The numbers 5 through 20 and the number 30 are declined in the following manner (note that the endings are the same as those for feminine nouns ending in a soft sign):

Nom.	шесть (6)	во́семь (8)	двена́дцать (12)	три́дцать (30)
Acc.	шесть	во́семь	двена́дцать	три́дцать
Gen.	шести́	восьми́	двена́дцати	тридцати́
Prep.	шести́	восьми́	двена́дцати	тридцати́
Dat.	шести́	восьми́	двена́дцати	тридцати́
Inst.	шестью́	восьмью́	двена́дцатью	три́дцатью

Example: Мы их жда́ли о́коло семи́ часо́в. (We waited for them about seven hours.)

Note that во́семь drops the -e- in all cases except the nominative and accusative. (The same occurs with 80 and 800.)

The numbers 50, 60, 70, and 80 also are declined in the same way, but both parts of these compound numbers must be declined. Fortunately, the same ending is used for both parts:

Nom.	шестьдеся́т (60)
Acc.	шестьдеся́т
Gen.	шести́десяти
Prep.	шести́десяти
Dat.	шести́десяти
Inst.	шестью́десятью

Example: У него́ не́ было семи́десяти до́лларов. (He didn't have seventy dollars.)

The numbers 40, 90, and 100 are quite easy to decline:

Nom.	со́рок	девяно́сто	сто
Acc.	со́рок	девяно́сто	сто
Gen.	сорока́	девяно́ста	ста
Prep.	сорока́	девяно́ста	ста
Dat.	сорока́	девяно́ста	ста
Inst.	сорока́	девяно́ста	ста

Example: Э́тому зда́нию о́коло ста лет. (That building is about one hundred years old.)

In 200, 300, 400, 500, 600, 700, 800, and 900, both parts of the compound must be declined. The first part of the number is declined like the corresponding single digit: for example, четыре- in четы́реста is declined exactly like четы́ре. Note that there are variations in the form of the second part of the compound. The nominative singular of 200 is две́сти, of 300, три́ста, of 600, шестьсо́т. This does not mean, however, that each number has its own forms. The numbers 300 and 400 take the same forms in all cases (for example, три́ста and четы́реста), and 500–900 take the same ones in all cases (пятьсо́т, шестьсо́т, etc.)

Nom.	две́сти (200)	три́ста (300)	шестьсо́т (600)
Acc.	две́сти	три́ста	шестьсо́т
Gen.	двухсо́т	трёхсот	шестисо́т
Prep.	двухста́х	трёхстах	шестиста́х
Dat.	двумста́м	трёмстам	шестиста́м
Inst.	двумяста́ми	тремяста́ми	шестьюста́ми

Example: Профе́ссор чита́л докла́д семиста́м студе́нтам. (The professor read a lecture to seven hundred students.)

Тысяча (one thousand) is declined like a feminine noun ending in -a. Миллио́н (one million) and миллиа́рд (one billion) are declined like masculine hard-stem nouns. Unlike other numbers, ты́сяча, миллио́н, and миллиа́рд never behave like adjectives—no matter what the case, they will always cause the noun that follows to be in the genitive:

> Он говори́л о ты́сяче вопро́сов. (He talked about a thousand issues.)

What happens when you want to say, for example, two thousand or five million? As stated above, ты́сяча, миллио́н, and миллиа́рд are declined as nouns. They will therefore be affected by a number in the same way as nouns:

> Здесь живу́т две ты́сячи (gen. sing.) жи́телей. (Two thousand people live here.)
> В э́той библиоте́ке пять миллио́нов (gen. plur.) книг. (There are five million books in this library.)

As you would expect, the genitive singular form is used after 2, 3, 4, and their compounds (ты́сячи, миллио́на, миллиа́рда) and the genitive plural is used after other numbers (ты́сяч, миллио́нов, миллиа́рдов).

When using compound cardinal numbers, remember that all elements must be declined:

> четы́рнадцать ты́сяч пятьсо́т се́мьдесят два (14,572) (nominative)
> четы́рнадцати ты́сяч пятиста́х семи́десяти двух (14,572) (prepositional)

It would appear from the above example that the use of numbers in Russian can be quite difficult for those who are learning the language. It can be difficult for native Russians as well, and they may avoid putting large numbers into any case other than the nominative or genitive. Students of Russian can do the same, but they need a recognition knowledge of numbers in the other cases.

When the presence of a cardinal number entails the use of a noun in the genitive case, a sentence may lose its subject in the nominative. Compare:

> Кни́ги (nom.) лежа́ли на столе́. (The books were lying on the table.)
> Пять книг (gen.) лежа́ли (or лежа́ло) на столе́. (Five books were lying on the table.)

One result of this loss is a possible change in the form of the verb. In the second example, the verb can remain the same or take a neutral form (neuter singular in the past tense, third-person singular in the present or future tense). Either option is acceptable.

Fractions

половина	one-half
треть	one-third
чётверть	one-quarter
две трети	two-thirds
три чётверти	three-quarters
полторá	one and one-half

As you might expect, the genitive case is required after fractions, too. The choice of singular or plural will depend on the meaning. For example:

Положи чётверть чáшки (**gen. sing.**) овощéй в суп. (Put one-quarter of a cup of vegetables into the soup.)
Половина людéй (**gen. plur.**) на собрáнии ушли рáно. (Half the people at the meeting left early.)

§14.2 ORDINAL NUMBERS

As you can see from §14.1, it is not easy to learn how to use cardinal numbers. Ordinal numbers, fortunately, are simpler. They always agree in gender, number, and case with the noun to which they refer, and they are declined like hard-stem adjectives. (Трéтий [third], however, does have an irregular declension; see below.)

пéрвый -ое, -ая, -ые	first
второй -ое, -ая, -ые	second
трéтий -ье, -ья, -ьи	third
четвёртый -ое, -ая, -ые	fourth
пятый -ое, -ая, -ые	fifth
шестой -ое, -ая, -ые	sixth
седьмой -ое, -ая, -ые	seventh

восьмо́й -ое, -ая, -ые	eighth
девя́тый -ое, -ая, -ые	ninth
деся́тый -ое, -ая, -ые	tenth
оди́ннадцатый -ое, -ая, -ые	eleventh
двена́дцатый -ое, -ая, -ые	twelfth
трина́дцатый -ое, -ая, -ые	thirteenth
четы́рнадцатый -ое, -ая, -ые	fourteenth
пятна́дцатый -ое, -ая, -ые	fifteenth
шестна́дцатый -ое, -ая, -ые	sixteenth
семна́дцатый -ое, -ая, -ые	seventeenth
восемна́дцатый -ое, -ая, -ые	eighteenth
девятна́дцатый -ое, -ая, -ые	nineteenth
двадца́тый -ое, -ая, -ые	twentieth
тридца́тый -ое, -ая, -ые	thirtieth
сороково́й -ое, -ая, -ые	fortieth
пятидеся́тый -ое, -ая, -ые	fiftieth
шестидеся́тый -ое, -ая, -ые	sixtieth
семидеся́тый -ое, -ая, -ые	seventieth
восьмидеся́тый -ое, -ая, -ые	eightieth
девяно́стый -ое, -ая, -ые	ninetieth
со́тый -ое, -ая, -ые	one hundredth
двухсо́тый -ое, -ая, -ые	two hundredth
трёхсотый -ое, -ая, -ые	three hundredth
четырёхсотый -ое, -ая, -ые	four hundredth

пятисо́тый -ое, -ая, -ые	five hundredth
шестисо́тый -ое, -ая, -ые	six hundredth
семисо́тый -ое, -ая, -ые	seven hundredth
восьмисо́тый -ое, -ая, -ые	eight hundredth
девятисо́тый -ое, -ая, -ые	nine hundredth
ты́сячный -ое, -ая, -ые	thousandth
миллио́нный -ое, -ая, -ые	millionth
миллиа́рдный -ое, ая, -ые	billionth

The numbers пе́рвый through четвёртый, седьмо́й,
сороково́й, ты́сячный, миллио́нный, and миллиа́рдный
are irregularly formed, but the other numbers are formed by
dropping the genitive ending (-и or -a) from the cardinal
form of the number and adding adjectival endings.

As stated earlier, тре́тий has an irregular declension:

	Masculine	**Neuter**	**Feminine**	**Plural**
Nom.	тре́тий	тре́тье	тре́тья	тре́тьи
Acc.	like nom. or gen.	тре́тье	тре́тью	like nom. or gen.
Gen.	тре́тьего		тре́тьей	тре́тьих
Prep.	тре́тьем		тре́тьей	тре́тьих
Dat.	тре́тьему		тре́тьей	тре́тьим
Inst.	тре́тьим		тре́тьей	тре́тьими

(The masculine and plural accusative will be like the genitive when the noun is animate, and like the nominative
when the noun is inanimate.)

In compound numbers, only the last digit is in the ordinal
form. The rest of the compound number consists of cardinal

forms. The cardinal forms are not declined; only the ordinal forms change:

> Кни́жный магази́н нахо́дится на сто три́дцать шесто́й у́лице. (The bookstore is on 136th Street.)

§14.3 COLLECTIVE NUMBERS

Collective numbers are used when the focus is not on discrete individuals or items, but on the collection of individuals or items taken together. They also have a number of special uses (see below).

дво́е	two
тро́е	three
че́тверо	four
пя́теро	five
ше́стеро	six
се́меро	seven
во́сьмеро	eight

о́ба	both (masc. and neuter)
о́бе	both (fem.)

Nom.	о́ба	о́бе	тро́е	пя́теро
Acc.	like nom. or gen.	like nom. or gen.	like nom. or gen.	like nom. or gen.
Gen.	обо́их	обе́их	трои́х	пятеры́х
Prep.	обо́их	обе́их	трои́х	пятеры́х
Dat.	обо́им	обе́им	трои́м	пятеры́м
Inst.	обо́ими	обе́ими	трои́ми	пятеры́ми

(The accusative will be like the genitive when the noun is animate, and like the nominative when the noun is inanimate.)

Дво́е and тро́е are declined in the same way. From че́тверо on, the numbers are declined in the same way.

Collective numbers also exist for 9 and 10, but they are rarely used. In general, the higher the collective number, the less frequent its use. Collectives do not form compound numbers.

All collective numbers (except о́ба and о́бе) are followed by genitive plural adjectives and nouns. О́ба and о́бе are followed by genitive plural adjectives and genitive singular nouns. They are used when referring to two things of the same type:

О́бе маши́ны стоя́т в гараже́. (Both cars are parked in the garage.)

Collectives are similar in meaning to cardinal numbers, but are more limited in use.

1. Дво́е, тро́е, and че́тверо are used with nouns that exist only in the plural. As these nouns do not have singular forms, they cannot take the genitive singular after the cardinal numbers два, три, and четы́ре. The use of collectives, which require the genitive plural, allows for a way out:

Я хочу́ купи́ть дво́е часо́в. (I want to buy two watches.)
У них че́тверо дете́й. (They have four children.)

2. Collectives are used with personal pronouns:

Их бы́ло ше́стеро. (There were six of them.)

3. They may also be used alone:

Пришли́ тро́е. (Three [people] came.)

4. Collective numbers can be used with substantivized adjectives:

Че́тверо учёных написа́ли э́ту рабо́ту. (Four scholars wrote this paper.)

5. They may be used when people or things are presented as a group or a collective, rather than as separate entities:

У нас бу́дет се́меро госте́й сего́дня на у́жин. (We're going to have seven guests for dinner today.)

When the presence of a collective number entails the use of a noun in the genitive case, a sentence may lose its subject in the nominative. Compare:

На стене́ висе́ли часы́. [nominative] (A clock hung on the wall.)
На стене́ висе́ли (or висе́ло) дво́е часо́в. [genitive] (Two clocks hung on the wall.)

One result of this loss is a possible change in the form of the verb. In the second example, the verb can remain the same or take a neutral form (neuter singular in the past tense and third-person singular in the present or future tense.) Either option is acceptable. Collectives used with pronouns, however, always take the neutral verb form: Нас бы́ло че́тверо. (There were four of us.)

§15.

Prepositions

§15.1
WHAT ARE PREPOSITIONS?

Prepositions are words that indicate how nouns or pronouns are related to other words in a sentence. They may refer to location, direction, or time.

§15.2
POSITION

Prepositions precede the nouns to which they refer or the adjectives that modify those nouns:

> Они пошли в э́тот большо́й магази́н за хле́бом. (They went to that big store for bread.)

§15.3
THE USE OF PREPOSITIONS

Prepositions require the nouns that follow them to take a certain case. The choice of case depends on the preposition. For example, a noun that follows без (without) must be in the genitive case:

> Он вы́шел без ша́пки. (He went out without a hat.)

(The prepositions themselves are invariable.)

Lists of prepositions are provided in the sections on cases (see §9.3-2 through §9.3-6). In the section on the instrumental, for example, a list of prepositions that take the instrumental is given. These lists will not be repeated here, but they (and the explanations that follow them) should be reviewed by the student at this point.

As you already know, some prepositions can take only one case, and others can take more than one. The latter group may present some problems. A summary chart of prepositions that take more than one case is provided below:

в in(to), to, on (in reference to time), at (in reference to time) + the accusative case	в in + the prepositional case
на on(to), to, for (in reference to time) + the accusative case	на on, at + the prepositional case

за behind, beyond, (in exchange) for, within (in reference to time) + *the accusative case*	за behind, beyond, for (in the sense of going to fetch something) + *the instrumental case*
под under + *the accusative case*	под under + *the instrumental case*
с off of, from + *the genitive case*	с with (in the sense of "together with") + *the instrumental case*

See §9.3-2 for a discussion of в, на, за, and под as well as an explanation of case use with these prepositions.

The meaning of с when used with the genitive is quite different from its meaning when used with the instrumental, so confusion with that preposition is less likely than with в, на, за, and под.

One other set of prepositions may also cause some problems. The prepositions на (for) and за (within), mentioned above, as well as the preposition чéрез (in, after) are sometimes used in time expressions with the accusative case. It is important to distinguish them from each other.

When indicating the duration of time that will pass *after* an action takes place, use the preposition на:

Тáня уéхала на недéлю. (Tanya went away for a week.)

In other words, the action in the sentence occurs first (she goes away), then the time span (a week) follows.

When indicating the duration of time that will pass *before* an action takes place, use the preposition чéрез:

Тáня вернётся чéрез недéлю. (Tanya will return in a week.)

In other words, the time span (a week) must pass before the action in the sentence occurs (she returns).

When indicating the duration of time within which something is accomplished, use the preposition за with a perfective verb:

Я прочитáла эту книгу за день. (I read that book within a day.)

For the use of other prepositions in time expressions, see §20 and §21.

Although there are many prepositions, there is a kind of order and consistency in their use. This is particularly evident when prepositions are used for location or direction. If you use в to indicate motion toward a particular place (Мы идём в магазин. [We're going to the store.]), you will also use в to indicate location at that place (Мы сейчáс в магазине. [We're now in the store.]). Further, if you use в, you will use из to indicate departure from that place (Мы вышли из магазина. [We walked out of the store.]). The following chart lists the prepositions that correspond and indicates the cases required with them:

Motion Toward	Location	Motion Away
в + the accusative	в + the prepositional	из + the genitive
на + the accusative	на + the prepositional	с + the genitive
к + the dative	у + the genitive	от + the genitive
под + the accusative	под + the instrumental	из-под + the genitive
за + the accusative	за + the instrumental	из-за + the genitive
до + the genitive		от + the genitive

Дéти пошли в шкóлу. Сейчáс они в шкóле. В три часá они придýт из шкóлы. (The children went to school. Right now they're in school. At three o'clock they will return from school.)

Он подошёл к окнý. Он постоял у окнá. Он отошёл от окнá. (He walked up to the window. He stood at the window for a while. He walked away from the window.)

The prepositions к, у, and от are used not only with physical locations and objects, as in the last example above (окнó), but also in connection with people. Use these prepositions when referring to a visit to a person or persons, for either personal or business reasons. Although the visit is made to a person's home or office, only the person, not the place, is mentioned in such constructions.

Лиза пошлá к врачý. Сейчáс онá у врачá. Скóро онá вернётся от врачá. (Liza went to the doctor. She's now at the doctor's. Soon she'll return from the doctor's.)

Мы пошли к Ивáновым в гóсти. Мы были у Ивáновых. Мы пóздно вернýлись от Ивáновых. (We went to visit the Ivanovs. We were at the Ivanovs'. We returned late from the Ivanovs'.)

The examples above are translated into English using the possessive (for example, the doctor's). But often the location itself must be named in the English, even though it is not named in the Russian: Вчерá мы были у них. (Yesterday we were at their house.)

Note the way verbs of motion are used in the above sentences. They are used with prepositions that indicate motion toward a place or motion away from a place. Other verbs, such as verbs of being (быть [to be]) or verbs of position (постоять [to stand]), are used with prepositions that indicate location.

It is important to remember that prepositions cannot be translated literally. In fact, sometimes a preposition is not used at all in Russian when the equivalent phrase in English requires a preposition. Cases in Russian can indicate the relationship between words without any need for prepositions. For example:

Она́ е́ла суп **ло́жкой**. [instrumental case]
    (She ate the soup *with a spoon.*)
Я дала́ газе́ту **А́нне**. [dative case]
    (I gave the paper *to Anna.*)
Мы бы́ли дово́льны **пое́здкой**. [instrumental case]
    (We were happy *with the trip.*)
Дире́ктор **заво́да** [genitive case] до́лго говори́л с рабо́чими.
    (The director *of the factory* talked with the workers for a long time.)

§16.

Conjunctions

Some commonly used conjunctions

и	and
а	and/but (see explanation below)
но	but
или	or
или . . . или	either . . . or
ни . . . ни	neither . . . nor
что	that
чтобы	(so) that, in order to
если	if
ли	if, whether
потому что	because
когда	when, while, after
пока	while, until
как	like, as

Conjunctions join words, clauses, or sentences. The conjunction и links words possessing some shared characteristics to form a series in the same way that "and" does in English. The words linked by any given conjunction и belong to the same category: that is, two or more nouns, pronouns, verbs, adjectives, adverbs, numbers, clauses, or sentences can be joined by и.

> Комната была большая и удобная. [adjectives] (The room was large and comfortable.)
> Он написал работу хорошо и быстро. [adverbs] (He wrote the paper well and quickly.)
> Коля, Маша и Лена ходили в библиотеку. [nouns] (Kolya, Masha, and Lena went to the library.)

In some instances и is used for emphasis, not for linkage. It is translated as "also, too" in such cases:

> И я хочу пойти на пляж! (I want to go to the beach, too!)

Note the word order—in such sentences и immediately precedes the word to be emphasized.

The conjunction а, sometimes translated as "but" and sometimes as "and," may also join words in the same category. The use of this conjunction, however, implies a contrast between the two components and places them in some kind of opposition to each other:

> Игорь работает, а Андрей отдыхает. (Igor is working and Andrei is resting.)
> Она не дома, а в университете. (She's not at home but at the university.)

This conjunction may also point out an unusual circumstance:

Бы́ло хо́лодно, а он вы́шел без пальто́. (It was cold, but he went out without a coat.)

The conjunction но suggests that there is a contradiction or that something is contrary to expectation. It reflects a stronger contrast than the conjunction а.

Она́ сказа́ла, что прие́дет, но не прие́хала. (She said that she would come, but she didn't.)

Мы мно́го рабо́тали, но ничего́ не ко́нчили. (We worked hard, but we didn't finish anything.)

The conjunction и́ли is used when a choice must be made between two possibilities.

Ты хо́чешь пойти́ в музе́й и́ли сиде́ть до́ма? (Do you want to go to the museum or stay home?)

Either . . . or is expressed by using и́ли . . . и́ли.

Он и́ли напи́шет и́ли позвони́т. (He will either write or call.)

The negation, neither . . . nor, is ни . . . ни:

У меня́ нет ни вре́мени, ни жела́ния э́то де́лать. (I have neither the time nor the inclination to do that.)

Э́ти де́ти не мо́гут ни чита́ть ни писа́ть. (These children can neither read nor write.)

Note that in addition to ни . . . ни, you must include не or нет in these sentences. The construction у меня́ нет in the first sentence above is simply the negation of у меня́ есть, and in the second example, the auxiliary verb is preceded by the negative particle не. In sentences with и́ли . . . и́ли or ни . . . ни, и́ли or ни must come immediately before the two elements in question (и́ли напи́шет и́ли позвони́т, ни чита́ть ни писа́ть).

As you already know, что has a number of functions. It is, among other things, a conjunction. When it is a conjunction, что is never stressed in the pronunciation of the sentence, as it is in its other uses.

Я зна́ю, что он вчера́ прие́хал. (I know that he arrived yesterday.)

In English, "that" can be omitted from such sentences; in Russian, however, что must always be included, except in extremely colloquial usage.

The conjunction что́бы indicates the purpose for which something is done. Like что, что́бы introduces a subordinate clause, but its use is somewhat more complicated. If the subject of both clauses is the same, then an infinitive must be used in the subordinate clause:

Он встал, что́бы уйти́. (He got up in order to leave.)

If the subjects of the two clauses are different, then the verb in the subordinate clause is in the past tense, regardless of the actual time of the action described:

> Я повезу детей в музей, чтобы они там провели день. (I'll take the children to the museum so that they can spend the day there.)

As in the case of что, чтобы is not optional and cannot be left out of a sentence. There is, however, one exception to this rule. When a verb of motion is used in the main clause, чтобы may be omitted.

> Она пошла домой, (чтобы) достать книги. (She went home to get her books.)

With verbs that indicate a wish, request, or demand, чтобы is used only when the subjects in the two clauses are different:

> Я хочу, чтобы ты ушёл. (I want you to leave.)

Note that, as before, the verb in the subordinate clause is in the past tense; the tense is not a reference to the actual time of the action described.

When the subject of the two clauses is the same, чтобы is eliminated and an infinitive is used:

> Я хочу уйти. (I want to leave.)

Чтобы is sometimes shortened to чтоб when the word that follows begins with a vowel.

The conjunction для того, чтобы may replace чтобы when there is a need to make the sentence more emphatic.

The conjunction если indicates the conditions that are required for an action to take place. It is used in complex sentences.

> Если я поеду в город, я там куплю книги (If I go to the city, I'll buy books there.)

The above use of если applies to real conditions. Если can also be used in conditional sentences to describe "unreal" conditions—that is, actions that could have occurred or may occur. See §12.3-3 and §12.9 for an explanation of the conditional mood.

The conjunction ли is worth mentioning in connection with если. The two words are similar, but not interchangeable.

Ли is used most often in indirect questions that require yes or no answers.

Compare:
a direct question—He asked me, "are you going?"
an indirect question—He asked me whether I was going.

Word order is particularly important when using ли: ли is always the second element in the clause in which it appears, while the word being questioned comes first (prepositions do not count as separate words in this context).

> Я не зна́ю, написа́ла ли Све́та рабо́ту. (I don't know whether Sveta wrote the paper.)
> Я не зна́ю, Све́та ли написа́ла рабо́ту. (I don't know whether Sveta wrote the paper.)

In the first example, the speaker wants to know whether the paper has been *written*. In the second, the speaker wants to know whether *Sveta* was the one who wrote it.

Since both е́сли and ли can be translated as "if," how can you tell when to use ли, when е́сли? The rule of thumb is this—if the sentence can be translated into English using "whether," then ли should be used in the Russian.

(Ли can also function as a particle, and as such, it can be used in direct questions that are answered yes or no:

> Бы́ли ли они́ в Ло́ндоне в про́шлом году́? [Were they in London last year?]

The rules for word order are the same as they are for ли when it is a conjunction.)

To indicate the reason for something, use the conjunction потому́ что. Like е́сли, it is used in complex sentences.

> Он не пришёл на уро́к, потому́ что он бо́лен. (He didn't come to class because he's sick.)

Use the conjunction когда́ to indicate the time at which something takes place. Pay particular attention to the aspect of the verbs in sentences with когда́: the meaning of this conjunction depends on the aspect.

1. If the verbs are imperfective in both clauses, then the action of the two verbs is simultaneous, and когда́ means "while":

> Когда́ она́ у́жинала, она́ смотре́ла телеви́зор. (She was watching television while she was eating dinner.)

2. If the verbs are perfective in both clauses, then the action of the two verbs is consecutive, and когда́ means "after":

> Когда́ она́ поу́жинала, она́ посмотре́ла телеви́зор. (After she ate dinner, she watched television.)

3. If the verb is imperfective in the subordinate clause and perfective in the main clause, then the two actions overlap and the perfective action "interrupts" the imperfective one. In such sentences, когда́ means "when":

> Когда́ Анто́н занима́лся в библиоте́ке, он встре́тил Та́ню. (When Anton was studying in the library, he ran into Tanya.)

The conjunction пока́ also indicates the time at which something takes place, but it is more limited in use, because it only means "while":

> На́до пойти́ погуля́ть, пока́ ещё светло́. (We should go for a walk while it's still light.)

When used with the negative particle не, пока́ means "until":

> Я бу́ду сиде́ть здесь, пока́ я не решу́ зада́чу. (I'm going to sit here until I solve the problem.)

Note that the particle не is not translated literally, and note also the word order: the particle не precedes the verb in the subordinate clause.

The conjunction как is used for comparative constructions in both simple and complex sentences.

> Ребёнок испуга́лся. Он был бе́лый, как полотно́. (The child was frightened. He was white as a sheet.)
> Мы пое́хали в дере́вню по́ездом, как вы сове́товали. (We went to the country on the train, as you suggested.)

§17.

Interjections

Interjections are words that indicate some kind of emotion felt by the speaker (but do not describe it).

Some commonly used interjections

ой	ow, ouch; oh (in reference to pain or fear)
ох	oh
ах	ah
эх	eh, oh
ай	oh (in reference to pain or fear); tut-tut
фу	ugh, ick, yuck
ура́	hurray
ого́	oho
ага́	aha
тс	shh
на	here, take [something]
алло́	hello

Some interjections express only one kind of emotion or convey only one kind of meaning, for example, тс, ура́, алло́, and фу. Others convey different emotions, and their meaning depends on the context in which they appear:

Ох, как я уста́ла! (Oh, I'm so tired!)
Ох, как стра́шно! (Oh, how frightening!)
Ох, како́й краси́вый вид! (Oh, what a beautiful view!)

Interjections are usually followed by a comma, as in the examples above, but they may also be followed by an exclamation point for special emphasis:

Фу! Кака́я невку́сная еда́! (Yuck! What horrible food!)
Ой! Мне бо́льно! (Ouch! That hurts!)

Special Topics

§18.

Word Formation

Words are not formed randomly or haphazardly—there are patterns in word formation. The ability to recognize these patterns makes it easier to learn new words, remember words, and translate sentences. The scope of this book does not allow for a lengthy presentation of the complex subject of word formation. What follows is a series of charts that present some of the most frequently encountered prefixes and suffixes in Russian.

Suffixes (for adjectives and nouns) and prefixes have certain general meanings, and their presence in a word helps to define that word. Prefixes and suffixes are attached to roots. A root is the central part of a word and gives the word its basic meaning. Some words have no prefixes or suffixes and consist only of the root: for example, стол (table). Other words may have a root and a prefix, or a root and a suffix. Some words have a root and both a prefix and a suffix.

	Prefix	Root	Suffix
ключик (small key)		ключ-	-ик
перенёс ([he] carried over)	пере-	-нёс	
безрабóтный (unemployed)	без	-рабóт-	-н(ый)

Prefixes come before the root and suffixes come after. When taken together, the prefix (if there is one), the root, and the suffix (if there is one) of a word are called a stem. Some words have more than one prefix, root, or suffix. For example, самолёт (airplane) contains the roots сам (self) and лёт (fly).

An ending is generally added to the end of a stem. Endings determine the way that a word is related to other words in a sentence. In the word лóжка (spoon), for example, the ending -a indicates that the word is in the nominative singular and is therefore the subject of the sentence in which it is found. In the word лóжку, on the other hand, the

179

ending -y indicates that the word is in the accusative singular and it is therefore a direct object.

Each part of speech has its own set of suffixes. The suffixes used for nouns, for example, are different from those used for adjectives.

Prefixes change the meanings of words but do not change parts of speech. For example, an adjective may experience a change in meaning by the addition of a prefix, but it remains an adjective. Prefixes are used most extensively with verbs.

Some Commonly Used Suffixes for Nouns

Suffix	General Meaning	Examples
-тель *(m.)* -тель+ниц(а) *(f.)*	Indicates a person's profession, occupation, or role.	учи́тель, учи́тельница (teacher) зри́тель, зри́тельница (spectator, onlooker)
-(н)ик *(m.)* -(н)иц(а) *(f.)* -(ч)ик / -(щ)ик *(m.)* -(ч)иц(а) / -(щ)иц(а) *(f.)*	Indicates a person's profession, occupation, role, or position.	перево́дчик, перево́дчица (translator) шко́льник, шко́льница (schoolchild) фи́зик (physicist) [Used for both males and females]
-ист *(m.)* -истк(а) *(f.)*	Indicates a person who belongs to a particular group or movement. May also indicate profession or occupation.	коммуни́ст, коммуни́стка (Communist) тури́ст, тури́стка (tourist) журнали́ст, журнали́стка (journalist)
-(а)тор	Indicates a person's profession or occupation.	дире́ктор (director) организа́тор (organizer)

-анин / -янин *(m.)* -анк(а) / -янк(а) *(f.)*	Indicates a person belonging to a particular nationality, ethnic group, or geographically determined category.	англича́нин, англича́нка (English person) киевля́нин, киевля́нка (resident of Kiev) граждани́н, гражда́нка (citizen)
-ец *(m.)* -к(а) *(f.)*	Same as above.	америка́нец, америка́нка (American)
-ич *(m.)* -ичк(а) *(f.)*	Same as above.	москви́ч, москви́чка (Muscovite [resident of Moscow])
-ин *(m.)* -к(а) *(f.)*	Same as above.	армяни́н, армя́нка (Armenian)
-онок / -ёнок	Indicates a young animal or human being.	ребёнок (child) котёнок (kitten)
-ость	Indicates an abstract quality of a person or thing.	мо́лодость (youth) сла́бость (weakness) мо́щность (power)
-изм	Is the equivalent of the English suffix *-ism*.	реали́зм (realism) социали́зм (socialism)
-ци(я)	Is the equivalent of the English suffix *-tion*.	конститу́ция (constitution) организа́ция (organization)
-ство	Indicates an abstract idea and/or the people who represent that idea.	госуда́рство (government) челове́чество (humanity) о́бщество (society)

-(e)ни(е) -(а)ни(е) -(я)ни(е)	Indicates a process that is connected with an action.	собра́ние (meeting) чте́ние (reading) упражне́ние (exercise)
-тие	Same as above.	заня́тие (activity, pastime)
-ок -ек -ик -ка -ко -чик	Creates a diminutive.	сыно́к (son) сто́лик (table) кни́жка (book) молочко́ (milk)

Some Commonly Used Suffixes for Adjectives

Suffix	General Meaning	Examples
-н- -енн- -онн-	An extremely common adjectival suffix used in qualitative and relational adjectives (used to form adjectives from inanimate nouns only).	вку́сный (delicious) свобо́дная (free) се́верное (northern) изве́стная (well-known) обще́ственное (social)
-ск-	An extremely common adjectival suffix used in relational adjectives (in reference to people, place names, abstractions, and technical terminology).	де́тский (child's) ру́сская (Russian) челове́ческое (human)
-ов-	An extremely common adjectival suffix used in relational adjectives (in reference to concrete nouns).	мирово́й (world) берёзовая (birch)
-еньк- -оньк-	Creates a diminutive.	ми́ленькая (nice)

Some Commonly Used Prefixes for Adjectives and Nouns

Prefix	General Meaning	Examples
не-	Indicates negation or the opposite of the original word.	небольшой (small) (the negation of большой [large]) независимость (independence) (the opposite of зависимость [dependence])
без-	Same as above.	безврéдный (harmless) (the opposite of врéдный [harmful])
со-	Indicates joint effort, equal participation, the combining or unification of elements. Sometimes translated as *co-*.	соединённая (united) сослуживец (co-worker)
под-	Indicates a subdivision or a lower position relative to someone or something else.	подсвéчник (candlestick) (i.e., that which goes under the candle [свéчка])
при-	Indicates attachment or connection.	пригород (suburb) (i.e., that which is attached to a larger urban area [гóрод])
пра-	Is the equivalent of the English *great-* (in the context of family relationships).	прабáбушка (great-grandmother)
пред-	Is the equivalent of the English *pre-*.	предназнáченный (predetermined)

на-	An extremely common prefix with a wide variety of uses and meanings.	назва́ние (name) науч́ный (scientific) налёт (raid)
над-	A prefix with a variety of uses and meanings.	на́дпись (inscription, sign) надзо́р (supervision)
из- ис-	Indicates using something up or producing something.	изда́ние (edition, publication)
анти-	Is the equivalent of the English *anti-*.	антикоммуни́ст (anti-Communist)

Prefixes are less important than suffixes for adjectives and nouns. For verbs, on the other hand, prefixes are very important. Verbal prefixes were discussed in the section on verbs of motion and will not be listed again here (see §12.11). Keep in mind that verbal prefixes can be used with nouns and adjectives as well. For example, the verbal prefix вы- applies to:

выходи́ть (verb—to go out)
вы́ход (noun—exit)
выходно́й [день] (adjective—day off)

§19.

Idioms

Idioms are set phrases or expressions that cannot be translated literally. It is necessary to know and recognize an idiom in order to translate it properly. Russian has quite a number of idiomatic expressions. Fortunately, books and dictionaries of idioms are available, and standard dictionaries also list some idioms under their key words. Two books on idioms are M. I. Dubrovin's *A Book of Russian Idioms Illustrated* and N. Shansky and E. Bystrova's *700 Russian Idioms and Set Phrases* (both by Russian Language Publishers).

When translating from Russian, keep the following rule of thumb in mind: if a sentence does not seem to make sense after it has been carefully translated, check for the possibility of an idiomatic expression.

Since there are so many idioms in Russian, only those that are most commonly used—and those that are more difficult to understand—will be given here. For a more comprehensive list, see one of the two books listed above.

Some idioms are common to English and Russian:

Взять быка́ за рога́. (To take the bull by the horns.)
Иска́ть иго́лку в сто́ге се́на. (To look for a needle in a haystack.)

Such idioms are easy to recognize and therefore will not be given here.

Idioms—Categorized by Subject Matter

Getting In and Out of Trouble

Idiom	Literal Meaning	Actual Meaning
Заварить кашу.	To cook kasha.	To cause trouble; to make a mess of things.
Сесть в лужу.	To sit down in a puddle.	To get oneself into trouble or into an awkward situation.
Ходить на голове́.	To walk on one's head.	To make trouble; to go wild (usually used in reference to children).
Заговаривать зубы.	To talk to (to charm) someone's teeth.	To talk one's way out of trouble.
Выйти сухим из воды.	To come out of the water dry.	To get out of trouble without facing any consequences.

Causing Trouble for Others

Idiom	Literal Meaning	Actual Meaning
Стоять над душой.	To stand over someone's soul.	To bother someone by standing over him or her, by hovering persistently.
Садиться на ше́ю.	To sit on someone's neck.	To make someone do what one wants.
Подложить свинью.	To lay down a pig.	To play a nasty trick on someone.
Выводить кого́-то из себя.	To lead someone outside of himself or herself.	To aggravate someone; to make him or her beside himself or herself.

Говорить под руку.	To speak under someone's hand.	To disturb someone's concentration or confidence when they are about to do something.
Давать кому-то сдачи.	To give someone change.	To give as good as one gets; to pay someone back.
Быть на ножах.	To be on knives.	To be angry and hostile toward one another.
Перемывать косточки.	To wash bones.	To gossip spitefully; to find fault.

One's Emotional State

Idiom	Literal Meaning	Actual Meaning
Быть не в своей тарелке.	To be not in one's own plate.	To be ill at ease; to feel out of place.
Вешать нос.	To hang one's nose.	To be discouraged.
Как в воду опущенный.	To be as if lowered into water.	To be depressed, dejected.
Лезть в бутылку.	To climb into a bottle.	To get irritated or angry, usually for no reason.
Кусать себе локти.	To bite one's elbows.	To be upset or sorry about a lost opportunity.
Выйти из себя.	To go out of oneself.	To lose control; to lose one's temper.
Взять себя в руки.	To take oneself in hand.	To pull oneself together.
Держать себя в руках.	To keep oneself in hand.	To restrain oneself; to pull oneself together.
В ус не дуть.	Not to blow into one's mustache.	Not to care at all.

Applying (or Not Applying) Oneself

Idiom	Literal Meaning	Actual Meaning
Делать что́-то спустя рукава́.	Working with one's sleeves rolled down.	Doing something without effort or attention.
Плева́ть в потоло́к.	To spit at the ceiling.	To do nothing; to waste time.
Тяжёл на подъём.	Heavy when going uphill.	To be slow and unwilling to get started.
Танцева́ть от пе́чки.	To start dancing from the stove.	To have to start things from the beginning in order to get them right.
Обива́ть поро́ги.	To knock against thresholds.	To go somewhere repeatedly in the persistent pursuit of something.
Разбива́ться в лепёшку.	To flatten oneself into a pancake.	To knock oneself out trying to achieve something.

Money Matters

Idiom	Literal Meaning	Actual Meaning
Жить на широ́кую но́гу.	To live on a wide foot.	To live well, spending money freely.
Влете́ть в копе́ечку.	To fly into a kopeck.	To spend a great deal of money for something.
Купи́ть кота́ в мешке́.	To buy a cat in a bag.	To buy something without knowing anything about its quality.
Вы́лететь в трубу́.	To fly out the chimney.	To lose all of one's money.

Figuring Things Out

Idiom	Literal Meaning	Actual Meaning
Ши́то бе́лыми ни́тками.	Sewn with white thread.	Something that is obvious or transparent.
Мота́ть себе́ на ус.	To wind something on one's mustache.	To observe something and to take it in; to make note of something.
Вот где соба́ка зары́та!	So that's where the dog is buried!	That's the essence of the matter; that's where the problem is.
Выводи́ть кого́-то на чи́стую во́ду.	To bring someone into clear water.	To bring someone out into the open; to expose his or her misdeeds.

Matters That Lack Substance

Idiom	Literal Meaning	Actual Meaning
Ви́лами на воде́ пи́сано.	Written with a pitchfork on water.	The prospects for something are extremely uncertain.
Вы́сосать что́-то из па́льца.	To suck something out of one's finger.	To make something up; to say something that has no substance.
Кот напла́кал.	A cat cried.	Something that does not amount to much.
Ни к селу́ ни к го́роду	Neither to the village nor to the city.	Something that does not fit, does not have a place, is irrelevant.
Перелива́ть из пусто́го в поро́жнее.	To pour something from one empty container into another.	To do something that is a complete waste of time.

Other Idioms

Idiom	Literal Meaning	Actual Meaning
Броса́ться кому́-то в глаза́.	To be thrown into someone's eyes.	To be noticeable, striking.
Глаза́ разбега́ются.	One's eyes run in different directions.	One does not know what to look at, what to focus on.
Идти́ куда́ глаза́ глядя́т.	To walk wherever one's eyes look.	To wander aimlessly.
Ве́ртится у кого́-то на языке́.	To spin on someone's tongue.	To have something on the tip of one's tongue.
Дли́нный язы́к.	A long tongue.	To be talkative.
Жить душа́ в ду́шу.	To live heart to heart.	To live in harmony.
Душа́ не лежи́т к чему́-то и́ли кому́-то.	One's heart does not lie toward something or someone.	One is not favorably disposed toward something or someone.
Па́лка о двух конца́х.	A stick with two ends.	Something that can have good and bad consequences.
Перегиба́ть па́лку.	To bend a stick.	To go too far; to overdo something.
Сади́ться не в свои́ са́ни.	To sit down in someone else's sleigh.	To do something for which one is not suited.
Сиде́ть ме́жду двух сту́льев.	To sit between two chairs.	To try to hold to two mutually exclusive positions at the same time.
Сиде́ть на чемода́нах.	To sit on one's suitcases.	To be ready to go.
Ехать за́йцем.	To ride like a hare.	To ride on mass transportation without paying one's fare.

Медве́дь на у́хо наступи́л.	A bear stepped on one's ear.	To be tone deaf.
Ку́рам на́ смех.	To make the chickens laugh.	Something that is extremely ridiculous or funny.
Стре́ляный воробе́й.	A sparrow that has been shot at.	A person who is very experienced and cannot be fooled.
Замори́ть червячка́.	To underfeed the worm.	To have a snack.
Бить ключо́м.	To bubble up like a spring.	To proceed at full speed.
Клин кли́ном вышиба́ть.	To drive out one wedge with another.	To counter one action by another, similar action; to fight fire with fire.
Ни пу́ха ни пера́.	Neither down nor feather.	Good luck!
Не фунт изю́му.	That's not a pound of raisins.	That's not an insignificant matter.

Examples.

Он весь день плева́л в потоло́к. (He wasted the whole day.)

Не загова́ривай мне зу́бы! (Don't try to get out of this!)

Они́ давно́ уже́ на ножа́х. (They've been hostile toward one another for a long time now.)

Мы зашли́ в магази́н, и глаза́ разбежа́лись. (We came into the store and didn't know what to look at first.)

Почему́ ты куса́ешь себе́ ло́кти? (Why are you so upset with yourself?)

§20.

Telling Time

(For a review of numbers, see §14.)

The Hours

1:00	час
2:00	два часá
3:00	три часá
4:00	четы́ре часá
5:00	пять часóв
6:00	шесть часóв
7:00	семь часóв
8:00	вóсемь часóв
9:00	дéвять часóв
10:00	дéсять часóв
11:00	одúннадцать часóв
12:00	двенáдцать часóв

To indicate one o'clock, час is sufficient—there is no need to write одúн. (When indicating one minute, however, be sure to add the number: однá минýта.)

As you might expect, the case rules for numbers apply in time expressions as well. After two, three, and four, час is in the genitive singular; after five through twelve, it is in the genitive plural. The same applies for minutes:

2 minutes	две минýты (gen. s.)
10 minutes	дéсять минýт (gen. pl.)

Telling time on the hour is fairly simple: just give the hour as it is listed in the chart above. Telling time between the hours is a bit more complicated. In Russian, the hour that *follows* is used to indicate the time, not the hour that has just passed. For example:

5:05 пять минýт шестóго (literally, five minutes of the sixth hour)

Note the word order and the case usage. The minutes are given first, and минýта is in the genitive plural, as it should be after the number five. The hour, which must be in ordinal form, is in the genitive *singular*. It is not followed by the word "hour."

After the half-hour mark, a different construction is used:

1:50 без десятú (минýт) два (literally, two o'clock without ten minutes)

The preposition без (without) must come before the minutes given. Без is a preposition that takes the genitive; therefore, the minutes are in the genitive case (and минýта is always in the genitive plural). The use of минýта is optional, but it is generally included when the number of minutes is less than five. The hour, which is in cardinal form, takes the nominative case and comes last in the construction. It is not followed by the word "hour."

The quarter-hour and half-hour marks have special terms: чётверть (quarter) and половина (half).

9:15	чётверть десятого
6:45	без чётверти семь
1:30	половина второго

Sometimes, especially in official contexts, the 24-hour clock is used. All hours after noon have 12 added to them (2 P.M.: 2 + 12 = 14). The minutes are given after the hour. The hour listed is the one that has *passed*.

4:25 P.M. шестнадцать часов двадцать пять минут

All numbers are cardinal in this construction. They are followed by час and минута, which will be in the genitive singular or plural, depending on the number. Чётверть and половина are not used in this construction.

Such a construction, in which the minutes follow the hour, is sometimes used with the 12-hour clock as well. It is, needless to say, easier to use than the other types of constructions given earlier. You will see all types, however, and should know how to use and recognize them all.

Time Expressions

Который час? (What time is it?)
Сколько сейчас времени? (What time is it?)
В котором часу? (At what time?)

Examples:

Который час? (What time is it?)
Без девяти одиннадцать. (10:51)

Сколько сейчас времени? (What time is it?)
Три часа. Нет, извините, уже десять минут пятого. (3:00. No, sorry, it's already 4:10.)

В котором часу вы уезжаете? В четыре часа? (At what time are you leaving? At 4:00?)
Нет, без чётверти девять. (No, at 8:45.)

В котором часу начинается фильм? (At what time does the film start?)
В половине восьмого. (At 7:30.)

In Russian, the day is not divided into A.M. and P.M. The following terms are used instead:

утро	morning (from approximately 5 A.M. to noon)
день	day (noon to approximately 5 P.M.)

вéчер	evening (from approximately 5 P.M. to midnight)
ночь	night (from midnight to approximately 5 A.M.)

Examples:

2 A.M.	два часá нóчи
3 P.M.	три часá дня
8 P.M.	вóсемь часóв вéчера
10 A.M.	дéсять часóв утрá

Noon and midnight can be designated by двенáдцать часóв or by пóлдень (noon) and пóлночь (midnight).

One final term should be mentioned here as well: полчасá means half an hour.

§21.

Dates, Days, Months, Seasons

Days of the Week (note the different genders)

понедéльник *(m.)* Monday
втóрник *(m.)* Tuesday
средá *(f.)* Wednesday
четвéрг *(m.)* Thursday
пя́тница *(f.)* Friday
суббóта *(f.)* Saturday
воскресéнье *(n.)* Sunday

Months of the Year (all are masculine)

янвáрь   January
феврáль   February
март   March
апрéль   April
май   May
ию́нь   June
ию́ль   July
áвгуст   August
сентя́брь September
октя́брь   October
ноя́брь   November
декáбрь   December

Seasons (note the different genders)

веснá   *(f.)* spring   веснóй   in the spring
лéто   *(n.)* summer   лéтом   in the summer
óсень   *(f.)* fall   óсенью   in the fall
зимá   *(f.)* winter   зимóй   in the winter

When stating the date, put it into the nominative case and use the ordinal form of the number. Put the month into the genitive case. Note the word order: the number comes first, then the month.

Сегóдня двенáдцатое апрéля. (Today is the 12th of April.)

The number takes the neuter gender because of a noun with which the number agrees and which is understood but not written:

Сегóдня двенáдцатое [числó **(date, number)**] апрéля.

Числó, however, is written when asking the date:

Какóе сегóдня числó? (What is today's date?)

When using compound numbers in ordinal form, remember that only the last element is written in ordinal form. The rest is in cardinal form:

Сегóдня двáдцать пя́тое октября́. (Today is the 25th of October.)

In order to indicate that something took place or will take place on a given date, use an ordinal number in the genitive case. The month should also be in the genitive:

Онá родилáсь седьмóго мáрта. (She was born on March 7th.)

When stating the day of the week, use the nominative case:

Сегóдня пя́тница. (Today is Friday.)

When indicating that something took place or will take place on a given day of the week, use the preposition в and the accusative case.

Он позвони́т в срéду. (He will call on Wednesday.)

The date and the day of the week may be combined in one statement. The same rules apply as apply when days and dates are stated separately:

Я прилечу́ в Рим в воскресéнье шестнáдцатого áвгуста. (I will arrive in Rome on Sunday, August 16th.)

If you want to indicate the week of an event, use the preposition на and the prepositional case:

Мы бы́ли там на прóшлой недéле. (We were there last week.)
На слéдующей недéле мы тóже тудá поéдем. (Next week we're going to go there again.)
На э́той недéле мы дóма. (This week we'll be at home.)

To state the month of an event, the preposition в and the prepositional case are required:

В февралé бы́ло мнóго снéга. (In February there was a lot of snow.)

As you can see, there are a number of complications involved in the usage of days and dates. You need to know which case to use for each type of construction, whether to use a preposition and, if so, which one, and whether to use an ordinal or a cardinal number. The format of each construction must be learned separately.

But perhaps the most unpleasant aspect of the subject of dates for beginning students is the year. In English, one reads the year as two two-digit numbers: nineteen ninety. In Russian, the year is read as a single four-digit number. This may make the number seem daunting, but when it is broken down into its component parts, it is fairly straightforward.

The ordinal form in the nominative case is used when stating the year:

тысяча девятьсо́т девяно́стый год (1990)

Год (year) is always included when giving the year.

To indicate that something took place or will take place in a particular year, use the preposition в and the prepositional case:

Она́ поступи́ла в университе́т в тысяча девятьсо́т во́семьдесят пя́том году́. (She entered the university in 1985.)

Note the special -у prepositional ending on год.

The year must be in the genitive case if the month or the day and month are also stated:

Они́ познако́мились в сентябре́ тысяча девятьсо́т се́мьдесят второ́го го́да. (They met in September of 1972.)
Они́ познако́мились тре́тьего сентября́ тысяча девятьсо́т се́мьдесят второ́го го́да. (They met on September 3, 1972.)

Fortunately, the year is often abbreviated in informal conversation and only the last two digits are used:

В во́семьдесят седьмо́м году́ бы́ло жа́ркое ле́то. (In '87 we had a hot summer.)

When the date is written in numerals, the day comes first, followed by the month and year:

26/5/82   (May 26, 1982)

The same order is used if the month is written out:

26-го ма́я 1982 г.   (May 26, 1982)

Note the abbreviations: г. for год and -го for два́дцать шесто́го (26th).

The various components given in this section can be combined into one very precise date:

Сего́дня понеде́льник два́дцать девя́тое ноября́ тысяча девятьсо́т девяно́сто пе́рвого го́да. (Today is Monday, November 29, 1991.)
Они́ прие́хали в четве́рг, четырнадцатого декабря́ тысяча девятьсо́т шестьдеся́т четвёртого го́да. (They arrived on Thursday, December 14, 1964.)

The prepositions от (from) and до (to, until), which take the genitive case, are used with dates to indicate time spans:

Мы бу́дем в отпуску́ от пятна́дцатого июля до второ́го а́вгуста. (We will be on vacation from July 15th to August 2nd.)

§22.

Talking about the Weather, Health

The Weather

Хо́лодно. О́чень хо́лодно.   (It's cold. It's very cold.)
Прохла́дно. О́чень прохла́дно.   (It's cool. It's very cool.)
Тепло́. О́чень тепло́.   (It's warm. It's very warm.)
Жа́рко. О́чень жа́рко.   (It's hot. It's very hot.)
Вла́жно. О́чень вла́жно.   (It's humid. It's very humid.)
Бу́дет гроза́.   (There's going to be a thunderstorm.)
Бу́дет дождь.   (It's going to rain.)
Моро́сит.   (It's drizzling.)
Идёт дождь.   (It's raining.)
Дождь льёт, как из ведра́. (It's raining heavily. [literally:
     The rain is pouring as if out of a bucket.])
Бу́дет снег.   (It's going to snow.)
Идёт снег.   (It's snowing.)
Ва́лит снег.   (It's snowing heavily.)
Кака́я сего́дня пого́да?   (How's the weather today?)
Пого́да чу́дная.   (The weather is wonderful.)
Пого́да хоро́шая.   (The weather is good.)
Пого́да плоха́я.   (The weather is bad.)
Пого́да ужа́сная.   (The weather is awful.)
Пого́да я́сная.   (The weather is clear.)
Пого́да со́лнечная.   (The weather is sunny.)
Пого́да о́блачная.   (The weather is cloudy.)
Пого́да дождли́вая.   (The weather is rainy.)
Тума́нно.   (It's foggy.)
Ве́трено.   (It's windy.)
Стано́вится жа́рко / хо́лодно.   (It's getting hot/cold.)
Моро́з.   (It's below freezing.)

Health

Я пло́хо себя́ чу́вствую.   (I don't feel well.)
Я бо́лен *(m.)*. / Я больна́ *(f.)*.   (I'm sick.)
Я заболе́л *(m.)*. / Я заболе́ла *(f.)*.   (I got sick.)
Что с ва́ми?   (What's wrong?)
Что у вас боли́т?   (Where does it hurt?)
У меня́ боли́т голова́.   (I have a headache.)
У меня́ боли́т живо́т.   (I have a stomachache.)
У меня́ боли́т спина́.   (My back hurts.)
У меня́ боля́т зу́бы.   (I have a toothache.)
Я простуди́лся *(m.)*. / Я простуди́лась *(f.)*.   (I caught a cold.)
У меня́ грипп.   (I have the flu.)
У меня́ температу́ра.   (I have a temperature.)
У меня́ на́сморк и ка́шель.   (I have a head cold and a cough.)
Я принима́ю лека́рство.   (I'm taking medication.)
Я ча́сто боле́ю.   (I get sick frequently.)
Вы здоро́вы?   (Are you well?)
Вы вы́здоровели?   (Have you recovered?)
Вы попра́вились?   (Have you recovered?)
Мне ста́ло лу́чше.   (I feel better.)
Вы хорошо́ вы́глядите.   (You look good.)

Appendix

Consonant Mutation

к →
т → ч
ц →

г →
д → ж
з →

с → ш
х →

ск → щ
ст →

м → м + palatalized л
п → п + palatalized л
б → б + palatalized л
ф → ф + palatalized л
в → в + palatalized л

л ▸ palatalized л
н → palatalized н
р → palatalized р

Irregular Nouns

Nouns that end in -мя

	Singular	Plural
Nom.	и́мя (name)	имена́
Acc.	и́мя	имена́
Gen.	и́мени	имён
Prep.	и́мени	имена́х
Dat.	и́мени	имена́м
Inst.	и́менем	имена́ми

Nouns that end in -анин / -янин

	Singular	**Plural**
Nom.	англича́нин (Englishman)	англича́не
Acc.	англича́нина	англича́н
Gen.	англича́нина	англича́н
Prep.	англича́нине	англича́нах
Dat.	англича́нину	англича́нам
Inst.	англича́нином	англича́нами

	Singular	**Plural**
Nom.	крестья́нин (peasant)	крестья́не
Acc.	крестья́нина	крестья́н
Gen.	крестья́нина	крестья́н
Prep.	крестья́нине	крестья́нах
Dat.	крестья́нину	крестья́нам
Inst.	крестья́нином	крестья́нами

Nouns that end in -онок / -ёнок

	Singular	**Plural**
Nom.	медвежо́нок (bear cub)	медвежа́та
Acc.	медвежо́нка	медвежа́т
Gen.	медвежо́нка	медвежа́т
Prep.	медвежо́нке	медвежа́тах
Dat.	медвежо́нку	медвежа́там
Inst.	медвсжо́нком	медвежатами

	Singular	**Plural**
Nom.	котёнок (kitten)	котя́та
Acc.	котёнка	котя́т
Gen.	котёнка	котя́т
Prep.	котёнке	котя́тах
Dat.	котёнку	котя́там
Inst.	котёнком	котя́тами

The nouns мать *and* дочь

	Singular	Plural
Nom.	мать (mother)	ма́тери
Acc.	мать	матере́й
Gen.	ма́тери	матере́й
Prep.	ма́тери	матеря́х
Dat.	ма́тери	матеря́м
Inst.	ма́терью	матеря́ми

	Singular	Plural
Nom.	дочь (daughter)	до́чери
Acc.	дочь	дочере́й
Gen.	до́чери	дочере́й
Prep.	до́чери	дочеря́х
Dat.	до́чери	дочеря́м
Inst.	до́черью	дочерьми́

The noun це́рковь *(the noun* любо́вь *follows the same pattern but lacks plural forms)*

	Singular	**Plural**
Nom.	це́рковь (church)	це́ркви
Acc.	це́рковь	це́ркви
Gen.	це́ркви	церкве́й
Prep.	це́ркви	церква́х
Dat.	це́ркви	церква́м
Inst.	це́рковью	церква́ми

Case Endings for Singular Nouns

	Masculine	**Neuter**	**Feminine** -а / -я	**Feminine** -ь
Nom. Sing.	—	-о / -е / -ё	-а / -я	— (-ь)
Acc. Sing.	inanimate nouns—like nom. / animate nouns—like gen.	like nom.	-у / -ю	like nom.
Gen. Sing.	-а / -я	-а / -я	-ы / -и	-и
Prep. Sing.	-е (-и) [for -ий masc. nouns]	-е (-и) [for -ие neuter nouns]	-е (и) [for -ия fem. nouns]	-и
Dat. Sing.	-у / -ю		-е (-и) [for -ия nouns]	-и
Inst. Sing.	-ом / -ем / -ём		-ой / -ей / -ёй	-ью

Case Endings for Plural Nouns

	Masculine	**Neuter**	**Feminine** -а/-я	**Feminine** -ь
Nom. Plur.	-ы / -и (-а / -я)	-а / -я	-ы / -и	-и
Acc. Plur.	inanimate nouns like nom. / animate nouns like gen.			
Gen. Plur.	-ов / -ев / -ёв -ей [for -ь nouns and ж, ч, ш, and щ nouns]	—	—	-ей
Prep. Plur.	-ах/-ях			
Dat. Plur.	-ам / -ям			
Inst. Plur.	-ами / -ями			

Case Endings for Long-form Adjectives

	Singular			**Plural**
	Masculine	**Neuter**	**Feminine**	
Nom.	-ый / -ий / -ой	-ое / -ее	-ая / -яя	-ые / -ие
Acc.	like nom. or gen.	-ое / -ее	-ую / -юю	like nom. or gen.
Gen.	-ого / -его		-ой / -ей	-ых / -их
Prep.	-ом / -ем		-ой / -ей	-ых / -их
Dat.	-ому / -ему		-ой / -ей	-ым / -им
Inst.	-ым / -им		-ой / -ей	-ыми / -ими

Endings for Short-form Adjectives

	Singular			Plural
	Masculine	Neuter	Feminine	
Nom.	—	-о	-а	-ы / -и

The Forms for Possessive Adjectives and Pronouns

	Singular			Plural
	Masculine	Neuter	Feminine	
Nom.	мой/наш	моё/наше	моя/наша	мой/наши
Acc.	like nom. or gen.	моё/наше	мою/нашу	like nom. or gen.
Gen.	моего / нашего		моей/нашей	моих/наших
Prep.	моём / нашем		моей/нашей	моих/наших
Dat.	моему́ / нашему		моей/нашей	моим/нашим
Inst.	мойм / нашим		моей/нашей	мойми/нашими

Твои (your, singular) and свои (one's own) are declined in the same way as мой (my). Ваш (your, plural and formal) is declined in the same way as наш (our).

The Forms for the Demonstrative Adjectives and Pronouns Э́тот (this, that) and То́т (that)

	Singular			Plural
	Masculine	**Neuter**	**Feminine**	
Nom.	э́тот / то́т	э́то / то	э́та / та	э́ти / те
Acc.	like nom. or gen.	э́то / то	э́ту / ту	like nom. or gen.
Gen.	э́того / того́		э́той / той	э́тих / тех
Prep.	э́том / том		э́той / той	э́тих / тех
Dat.	э́тому / тому́		э́той / той	э́тим / тем
Inst.	э́тим / тем		э́той / той	э́тими / те́ми

The Forms for the Interrogative Adjective and Pronoun Че́й (whose)

	Singular			Plural
	Masculine	**Neuter**	**Feminine**	
Nom.	че́й	чьё	чья́	чьи́
Acc.	like nom. or gen.	чьё	чью́	like nom. or gen.
Gen.	чьего́		чье́й	чьи́х
Prep.	чьём		чье́й	чьи́х
Dat.	чьему́		чье́й	чьи́м
Inst.	чьи́м		чье́й	чьи́ми

The Forms for Кто (who) and Что (what)

Nom.	кто	что
Acc.	кого́	что
Gen.	кого́	чего́
Prep.	ком	чём
Dat.	кому́	чему́
Inst.	кем	чем

The Reflexive Pronoun Себя (myself, yourself, himself, itself, herself, ourselves, yourselves, or themselves)

Nom.	———
Acc.	себя
Gen.	себя
Prep.	себе́
Dat.	себе́
Inst.	собо́й

The Forms for Intensive Pronouns in the Nominative Case

Masculine	Neuter	Feminine	Plural
сам	само́	сама́	са́ми

(In the other cases, they take standard long-form adjectival endings.)

Personal Pronouns

	Singular	Plural
First Person	я (I)	мы (we)
Second Person	ты (you)	вы (you)
Third Person	он, оно́, она́ (he, it, she)	они́ (they)

The Forms for Personal Pronouns

Singular					
			Masculine	**Neuter**	**Feminine**
Nom.	я	ты	он	оно́	она́
Acc.	меня	тебя	его́		её
Gen.	меня	тебя	его́		её
Prep.	мне	тебе́	нём		ней
Dat.	мне	тебе́	ему́		ей
Inst.	мной	тобо́й	им		ей (е́ю)

Plural			
Nom.	мы	вы	они́
Acc.	нас	вас	их
Gen.	нас	вас	их
Prep.	нас	вас	них
Dat.	нам	вам	им
Inst.	на́ми	ва́ми	и́ми

Endings for Past Tense Verbs

Singular			Plural
Masculine	**Neuter**	**Feminine**	
-л	-ло	-ла	-ли

Endings for Present Tense Verbs and for Perfective Future Tense Verbs

	1st Conjugation	2nd Conjugation
я	-у	(j) -у
ты	-ешь	-ишь
он, онó, онá	-ет	-ит
мы	-ем	-им
вы	-ете	-ите
они́	-ут	-ат/ ят

The Auxiliary Verb Быть (to be) Used with Imperfective Future Tense Verbs

я бýду
ты бýдешь
он, онó, онá бýдет
мы бýдем
вы бýдете
они́ бýдут

LET'S REVIEW
Test Yourself

§1. THE RUSSIAN ALPHABET

1. How many letters are there in the Russian alphabet?

   _____

2. The letter ж is pronounced like the highlighted letter in
   A. **z**oo   ☐
   B. **g**o   ☐
   C. mea**s**ure   ☐

3. The letter с is pronounced like the highlighted letter(s) in
   A. **c**ar   ☐
   B. **s**un   ☐
   C. **ch**ase   ☐

4. The letter в is pronounced like the highlighted letter in
   A. **v**erse   ☐
   B. **b**ook   ☐
   C. **d**og   ☐

5. The letter ф is pronounced like the highlighted letter(s) in
   A. **sh**ape   ☐
   B. **f**un   ☐
   C. **h**at   ☐

6. The letter й is pronounced like the highlighted letter(s) in
   A. to**y**   ☐
   B. **p**ig   ☐
   C. **y**arn   ☐

7. The letter д is pronounced like the highlighted letter in
   A. **b**ake   ☐
   B. **s**un   ☐
   C. **d**og   ☐

8. The letter ё is pronounced like the highlighted letter(s) in
   A. **yo**ur   ☐
   B. **ye**ll   ☐
   C. **you**   ☐

9. The letter щ is pronounced like the highlighted letter(s) in
   A. **ch**ase   ☐
   B. di**sh ch**ips   ☐
   C. mea**s**ure   ☐

§2. THE SPELLING RULES

10. The letter ы can be written after the letter ч.
    True or false? _____
11. The letter ю can be written after the letter к.
    True or false? _____
12. The letter и can be written after the letter щ.
    True or false? _____
13. The letter я can be written after the letter ж.
    True or false? _____
14. The letter у can be written after the letter х.
    True or false? _____
15. The letter а can be written after the letter ш.
    True or false? _____
16. The letter я can be written after the letter г.
    True or false? _____
17. The letter ю can be written after the letter ц.
    True or false? _____
18. The letter а can be written after the letter ц.
    True or false? _____
19. The letter е can be written after the letter ч.
    True or false? _____
20. An unstressed o can appear after the letter ж.
    True or false? _____
21. An unstressed o can appear after the letter ш.
    True or false? _____

§3. PRONUNCIATION

22. When unstressed and following a soft consonant, the
    letter я is pronounced like
    A. и ☐
    B. ы ☐
    C. a ☐
23. The pronunciation of the letter ю is unaffected by
    stress. True or false? _____
24. The letter ё is always stressed. True or false? _____
25. The following is an example of a soft vowel.
    A. o ☐
    B. e ☐
    C. у ☐
    D. a ☐

26. The following is an example of a hard vowel.
    A. и ☐
    B. я ☐
    C. е ☐
    D. у ☐
27. The soft sign and the hard sign cannot be written after vowels. True or false? _____
28. The following is an example of a voiced consonant.
    A. д ☐
    B. п ☐
    C. к ☐
    D. с ☐
29. The following is an example of a voiceless consonant.
    A. б ☐
    B. з ☐
    C. ф ☐
    D. в ☐
30. If the second consonant in a consonant cluster is voiced, the first consonant will be pronounced as voiced (provided it has a voiced counterpart). True or false? _____
31. The consonants л, м, р do not have voiceless counterparts. True or false? _____
32. When г occurs in the ending -ого, it is pronounced like в. True or false? _____
33. Perfective verbs with the prefix вы- are never stressed on the prefix. True or false? _____

§4. MECHANICS

34. The following is the correct way to write "German language" in Russian.
    A. неме́цкий язы́к ☐
    B. Неме́цкий язы́к ☐
    C. Неме́цкий Язы́к ☐
35. The following is the correct way to write "Tuesday" in Russian.
    A. Вто́рник ☐
    B. вто́рник ☐
36. The following is the correct way to write the title of the book, *Crime and Punishment*, in Russian.
    A. Преступле́ние и наказа́ние ☐
    B. Преступле́ние и Наказа́ние ☐

37. Which of the following words is divided into syllables incorrectly?
    A. во-да́   ☐
    B. по́л-ка   ☐
    C. ле́-йка   ☐

38. Which of the following words is divided into syllables incorrectly?
    A. бу́л-ка   ☐
    B. о́ко-ло   ☐
    C. ре-ка́   ☐

39. —Что э́то? The dash at the beginning of this question indicates that it is part of a dialogue. True or false?

    _____

§5. THE ABSENCE OF ARTICLES

40. Because there are no definite and indefinite articles in Russian, it is sometimes hard to say whether "a" or "the" should be used when translating a Russian sentence into English. True or false? _____

§6. THE ABSENCE OF THE VERB "TO BE" IN THE PRESENT TENSE

41. The verb быть is usually not written in the present tense in Russian. True or false? _____

42. Most forms of быть do not exist in the present tense. True or false? _____

43. The following is the correct way to write "I have money" if it is necessary to underscore the *existence* of the money.
    A. У меня́ де́ньги   ☐
    B. У меня́ есть де́ньги   ☐

Translate the following into Russian.

44. This is a school. _____

45. Maksim is a good doctor. _____

46. That's Natasha. _____

§7. WORD ORDER

47. In which position do interrogative words go in a
    sentence?
    A. first ☐
    B. second ☐
    C. last ☐
48. Word order in sentences is freer in English than in
    Russian. True or false? _____

§8. NAMES AND THE USE OF ТЫ AND ВЫ

49. A patronymic is the same as a middle name. True or
    false? _____
50. The father's name is used to form patronymics for both
    sons and daughters. True or false? _____
51. The patronymic is used in
    A. informal situations ☐
    B. formal situations ☐
52. Russian last names are difficult for students of Russian
    because
    A. some of the case endings are adjectival ☐
    B. all of the case endings are adjectival ☐

---

53. Fill in the following chart.

NOMINATIVE	masculine singular	Смирнóв
PREPOSITIONAL	masculine singular	_____
PREPOSITIONAL	feminine singular	_____
PREPOSITIONAL	plural	_____

Fill in the blanks by putting the words in parentheses
into the correct case.

54. Я идý к _____. (Иванóвы)
55. Мы вúдели _____. (Жукóвский)

Form patronymics using the names given in parentheses.

56. Николай _____. (Владимир)
57. Мария _____. (Пётр)
58. Нина _____. (Андрей)

> When introduced to the following people, which form
> of address would you use?

59. the 12-year-old daughter of a friend
    A. ты and name and patronymic   ☐
    B. ты and first name or nickname   ☐
    C. вы and first name   ☐
60. the father of your college classmate
    A. ты and first name   ☐
    B. вы and first name   ☐
    C. вы and name and patronymic   ☐

§9. NOUNS

> Translate the following words into Russian, giving both
> the nominative singular and the nominative plural forms.
> Note the gender of each word.

	Gender	Nominative Singular	Nominative Plural
61. museum			
62. metro			
63. week			
64. window			
65. newspaper			
66. grandfather			
67. day			
68. night			
69. chair			
70. shore			
71. money			
72. child			

> Fill in the blanks by putting the words in parentheses into the correct case.

73. Я вижу _____. (Иван)
74. Мы смотрели _____. (телевизор)
75. Они забыли _____. (билеты)
76. Лена купила _____. (молоко)
77. Мы проехали _____. (миля)

> Fill in the blanks by translating the words in parentheses and putting them into the correct case.

78. Саша пойдёт _____. (to the post office)
79. Потом он пойдёт _____. (to the store)
80. А Коля пойдёт _____. (to the beach)
81. Мы уедем _____. (in a month)
82. Я поставила зонт _____. (behind the door)
83. Учитель _____. (complained about you)
84. Дети _____. (play soccer)

> Fill in the blanks by putting the words in parentheses into the correct case.

85. В магазине не было _____. (вино)
86. Здесь много _____. (люди)
87. Книга интереснее _____. (фильм)
88. Я не хочу терять _____. (время)

> Fill in the blanks by translating the words in parentheses and putting them into the correct case.

89. Ты боишься _____? (dogs)
90. У меня нет _____. (money)
91. Это дом _____. (of my sister)
92. Катя съела _____. (some soup)

93. Ско́лько _____ ты купи́ла?
    (books)
94. Когда́ ко́нчилась ле́кция _____?
    (of the professor)
95. Мы бу́дем в Ло́ндоне _____.
    (approximately a week)
96. Э́то бы́ло _____. (after the
    war)

Fill in the genitive singular and the genitive plural
forms for the words listed below. Note the gender of
each word.

	Gender	Nominative Singular	Nominative Plural
97. ла́мпа			
98. де́рево			
99. врач			
100. иде́я			
101. брат			
102. зда́ние			

Fill in the blanks by translating the words in parentheses and putting them into the correct case.

103. Мы бы́ли _____. (in the forest)
104. Мы бы́ли _____. (in the library)
105. Ди́ма смотре́л програ́мму_____.
     (about the elections)
106. Он хорошо́ _____ (plays the piano)
107. Я бу́ду _____ в час. (at the station)
108. Не говори́ об э́том _____
     (in the presence of the children)
109. Ли́за ду́мает _____. (about Maksim)
110. Мари́на рабо́тает _____. (at the post
     office)

Fill in the prepositional singular and the prepositional plural forms for the words listed below. Note the gender of each word.

	Gender	Prepositional Singular	Prepositional Plural
111. и́мя			
112. це́рковь			
113. дочь			
114. сын			

Fill in the blanks by translating the words in parentheses and putting them into the correct case.

115. Он пи́шет письмо́ _____. (to Anna)
116. Студе́нты подошли́ _____.
(to the laboratory)
117. Я позвоню́ _____. (the teachers)
118. _____ не хо́чется занима́ться.
(Boris)
119. _____ бы́ло интере́сно посмотре́ть
э́тот фильм. (Grandmother)
120. Мы благода́рны _____. (to the doctors)
121. _____ написа́ть докла́д.
(the professor needs [use dative])
122. Шёл дождь и _____ игра́ть
в саду́. (the children couldn't [use dative])

Fill in the dative singular and the dative plural forms for the words listed below. Note the gender of each word.

	Gender	Dative Singular	Dative Plural
123. друг			
124. сосе́д			
125. котёнок			
126. муж			

Fill in the blanks by translating the words in parentheses and putting them into the correct case.

127. Он рабо́тает _____. (teacher)
128. Я хочу́ ко́фе _____. (with milk)
129. Пиши́ упражне́ния _____.
     (with a pencil)
130. Она́ ста́ла _____. (engineer)
131. Туда́ мо́жно прое́хать _____. (by bus)
132. _____ стои́т стол. (between
     the windows)
133. Са́ша говори́т _____.
     (in a quiet voice)
134. Ешь суп _____ (with a spoon)

Fill in the instrumental singular and the instrumental plural forms for the words listed below. Note the gender of each word.

	Gender	**Instrumental Singular**	**Instrumental Plural**
135. любо́вь			
136. и́мя			
137. лю́ди			
138. лист			

Fill in the blanks by translating the words in parentheses and putting them into the correct case.

139. Она́ принесла́ мно́го _____. (books)
140. За́втра я бу́ду _____. (in the city)
141. Де́ти бе́гают _____. (in the street)
142. Я забы́ла купи́ть _____. (milk)
143. Ко́ля занима́ется _____. (mathematics)
144. _____ стои́т в углу́. (table)
145. Мы прошли́ _____. (by the theater)
146. Дай _____ газе́ту. (Sasha)

§10. ADJECTIVES

Translate the following into Russian.

147. a small chair _____
148. a beautiful painting _____
149. a young man _____

Put each of the translations above into the cases given below.

150. a small chair (inst. plural) _____
151. a beautiful painting (gen. singular)_____
152. a young man (dat. singular) _____

Give the short forms for the following adjectives.

153. большо́й _____

154. больно́й _____

Using the appropriate до́лжен construction, translate the following sentence.

155. I need to read. _____

Using the appropriate form of the short adjective ну́жен, translate the following sentence.

156. He needed advice. _____

Translate the following into Russian, and put into the cases given.

157. our house (dat. singular) _____

158. my letter (inst. singular) _____

159. her sister (prep. singular) _____

160. your [plural or formal] books (gen. plural)

_____

161. one's own room (nom. singular)_____

162. this tree (acc. singular) _____

163. this lamp (inst. singular) _____

164. this boy and that girl (nom. singular) _____

_____

Translate the following sentences into Russian.

165. Whose car is in the street? _____

166. Whose notebooks are lying on the table? _____

167. Whose pencil? _____

Translate the following into Russian, using a simple comparative adjective.

168. that trip is more interesting _____

_____

> Translate the following into Russian, using a compound comparative adjective.

169. a newer airplane _____

> Translate the following into Russian, using the irregular compound comparative form.

170. the older brother _____

> Translate the following into Russian, using a simple superlative adjective.

171. a very great poet _____

> Translate the following into Russian, using a compound superlative adjective.

172. the best university _____

> Translate the following into Russian, using the superlative construction that takes всех.

173. He works more than everybody else. _____
_____

> Translate the following into Russian.

174. living room _____
175. adult _____
176. sick person _____

§11. PRONOUNS

> Translate the following sentences into Russian.

177. They were with us. _____
178. Did he give you [singular] the money? _____
_____
179. We talked about him. _____
180. What are you [singular] thinking about? _____
_____
181. I read the article that you wrote. _____
_____

182. I don't recognize myself. _____
_____

183. We did everything ourselves. _____
_____

184. Did anyone pass the exam? _____
_____

185. Something is lying on the shelf. _____
_____

186. We didn't see anyone. _____

§12. VERBS

Check the imperfective verb in each of the following verb pairs.

187. **A.** ко́нчить ☐   **B.** конча́ть   ☐
188. **A.** одева́ть ☐   **B.** оде́ть   ☐
189. **A.** крича́ть ☐   **B.** кри́кнуть   ☐
190. **A.** посиде́ть ☐   **B.** сиде́ть   ☐

Fill in the blanks by choosing the appropriate aspect for each sentence and putting the verb into the correct form. Use the past tense.

191. Он до́лго _____ .
(чита́ть/прочита́ть)
192. Студе́нты _____ зада́чи и
пошли́ домо́й. (реша́ть/реши́ть)
193. Она́ ча́сто _____ кни́ги из
библиоте́ки. (брать/взять)
194. Де́ти вдруг _____ .
(смея́ться/засмея́ться)
195. Ученики́ не _____
сочине́ние. Они́ не хоте́ли занима́ться.
(писа́ть/написа́ть)
196. Са́ша _____ к нам днём.
Сейча́с он до́ма. (приходи́ть/прийти́)
197. Она́ начала́ _____ в де́вять
часо́в. (рабо́тать/порабо́тать)

Put the following infinitives into the required **past tense forms.**

198. (игра́ть) он _____
199. (везти́) они́ _____
200. (идти́) он _____

201. (привы́кнуть) он _____
202. (мочь) она́ _____
203. (упа́сть) оно́ _____
204. (есть) они́ _____
205. (нача́ть) она́ _____
206. (отвеча́ть) он _____
207. (печь) они́ _____

Put the following infinitives into the required **present** tense forms.

---

208. (лета́ть) они́ _____
209. (ви́деть) я _____
210. (ждать) мы _____
211. (встава́ть) вы _____
212. (танцева́ть) она́ _____
213. (пить) они́ _____
214. (петь) ты _____
215. (жить) он _____
216. (е́хать) мы _____
217. (мочь) вы _____
218. (расти́) оно́ _____
219. (хоте́ть) мы _____
220. (бежа́ть) я _____

Put the following infinitives into the required **future** tense forms.

---

221. (закрыва́ть) он _____
222. (поду́мать) они́ _____
223. (ждать) вы _____
224. (получи́ть) ты _____
225. (сде́лать) мы _____
226. (позвони́ть) она́ _____
227. (дать) вы _____
228. (встать) я _____
229. (приня́ть) они́ _____
230. (сесть) мы _____

Translate the following sentences into Russian.

---

231. He wants to work. _____
232. Andrei knows how to swim. _____
233. We can help. _____
234. They finished studying at seven. _____

Form the singular/informal variant of the imperative for the following infinitives.

235. звони́ть _____

236. ду́мать _____

237. дать _____

238. узнава́ть _____

Form the plural/formal variant of the imperative for the following infinitives.

239. лечь _____

240. встать _____

Form the first person imperative for the following infinitive.

241. танцева́ть _____

Form the third person imperative, using **она́**, for the following infinitive.

242. рабо́тать _____

Translate the following sentences into Russian.

243. He would have passed the exam if he had studied.

_____

244. If I go to Paris, I will buy perfume. _____

_____

Put the following infinitives into the required **present** tense forms.

245. (улыба́ться) она́ _____

246. (мы́ться) я _____

Fill in the blanks by choosing the appropriate verb of motion for each sentence and putting the verb into the correct form. Use the **present** tense.

247. Де́ти _____ в шко́лу
ка́ждый день. (идти́/ходи́ть)

248. Я сейча́с _____ в магази́н
Что купи́ть? (е́хать/е́здить)

> Fill in the blanks by choosing the appropriate verb of motion for each sentence and putting the verb into the correct form. Use the **past** tense.

249. Вчерá Пáвел _____ Кóлю в гóрод. (везти́/вози́ть)

250. В прóшлом годý мы чáсто_____ в Москвý. (летéть/летáть)

251. To indicate movement out of an enclosed space, use the following prefix.
    A. в- ☐
    B. вы- ☐
    C. вз- ☐
    D. пере- ☐

252. To indicate movement away from someone or something, use the following prefix.
    A. при- ☐
    B. под- ☐
    C. от- ☐
    D. до- ☐

253. To indicate movement around someone or something, use the following prefix.
    A. об- ☐
    B. у- ☐
    C. с- ☐
    D. про- ☐

254. To indicate stopping at a place on the way to somewhere else, use the following prefix.
    A. раз- ☐
    B. в- ☐
    C. за- ☐
    D. под- ☐

> Translate the following sentences into Russian.

255. He sat down to the table. _____

256. Every evening Katya goes to bed at ten. _____
    _____

257. A beautiful vase is standing on the shelf. _____
    _____

258. They're sitting at the table in the corner . _____
    _____

259. Your coat is hanging in the closet. _____
    _____

260. Who hung up my coat in the closet? _____

261. I always put the newspapers on the shelf. _____

262. In the spring Ivan plants flowers. _____

> Identify each of the following participles by type (for example, "present active participle").

263. читáвшая _____

264. решáемые _____

265. решáемы _____

266. говоря́щий _____

267. брóшенное _____

> Form verbal adverbs (gerunds) from the following infinitives.

268. посмотрéть _____

269. сидéть _____

§13. ADVERBS

> Fill in the blanks with adverbs by translating the words in parentheses.

270. Пóезд идёт _____. (fast)

271. Ири́на _____ игрáет на роя́ле. (badly)

272. Мы пошли́ _____. (downstairs)

273. Они́ бу́дут ждать _____. (inside)

274. Мы пое́дем на дáчу _____.
(in the summer)

275. _____ шёл снег. (at night)

276. Они́ _____ хóдят в ресторáны. (rarely)

277. На пля́же я _____
отдыхáла. (a great deal)

278. Ни́на _____ забы́ла о лéкции.
(completely)

279. Эти брюки _____ мáленькие. (too)

280. Мы _____ бы́ли. (there)

281. _____ ты опоздáл? (why)

§14. NUMBERS

> Translate the following, writing all numbers in Russian.

282. 37 _____
283. 561 _____
284. 2,894 _____
285. 10,000 _____
286. 2,000,000 _____
287. 18 rooms _____
288. three days _____
289. 75 books _____
290. 21 professors _____
291. 40 houses _____
292. four new students _____
293. 15 big cars _____
294. 89 beautiful paintings _____
295. 36 old lamps _____
296. 67 small children _____
297. two (masc., neuter, and fem. forms)

_____

298. one (masc., neuter, fem., and plural forms)

_____

299. He was there alone. _____
300. Some students came to the lecture, others didn't.

_____

301. two-thirds _____
302. one-half _____
303. seventeenth _____
304. third _____
305. the second time _____
306. Eighth Street _____
307. the fifty-sixth floor _____
308. both newspapers _____
309. both magazines _____
310. there were four of us _____
311. three children _____

§15. PREPOSITIONS

> Fill in the blanks by translating the words in parentheses.

312. Игорь пошёл в магазин _____. (for milk)
313. Они уéхали _____. (for a day)

314. Он вернётся _____. (in a week)
315. Она написала статью _____.
(within a month)
316. Учительница подошла _____.
(to the blackboard)
317. Олег был _____. (at the doctor's)

§16. CONJUNCTIONS

> Fill in the blanks with conjunctions by translating the
> words in parentheses.

318. _____ мы были в театре, мы встретили
Ивановых. **(when)**
319. Я не пошла в парк, _____ _____ было холодно.
(because)
320. _____ не поздно, Вася пойдёт в библиотеку.
(while)
321. Мы купили билеты, _____ не пошли на оперу.
(but)
322. _____ я поеду на почту, я куплю тебе марки.
(if)
323. Я не знаю, буду _____ ____ я на собрании.
(whether)

§17. INTERJECTIONS

> Fill in the blanks with interjections by translating the
> words in parentheses.

324. ____ _____ ! Вот где мой ключи. **(aha)**
325. _____ ____! Фильм начался. **(shh)**

§18. WORD FORMATION

326. -тель is a suffix for
A. adjectives   ☐
B. nouns   ☐
327. -ск- is a suffix for
A. adjectives   ☐
B. nouns   ☐
328. -анин is a suffix for
A. adjectives   ☐
B. nouns   ☐

329. без- is a prefix for nouns and adjectives that indicates
    A. the negation or opposite of the original word   ☐
    B. attachment or connection   ☐

§19. IDIOMS

330. The idiomatic expression, заварить кашу, **means**
    A. to make a mess of things   ☐
    B. to talk one's way out of trouble   ☐
    C. to go wild   ☐
331. The idiomatic expression, кусать себе локти, **means**
    A. to feel out of place   ☐
    B. to lose control   ☐
    C. to be upset or sorry about a lost opportunity   ☐
332. The idiomatic expression, давать кому-то сдачи, **means**
    A. to do nothing   ☐
    B. to give as good as one gets   ☐
    C. to go too far   ☐

§20. TELLING TIME

> Write out the following times in Russian.

333. 9:00 _____
334. 2:45 _____
335. 11:50 _____
336. 5:05 _____
337. 4:00 _____
338. 7:30 _____
339. 8:48 _____
340. 1:00 _____
341. 3:20 _____
342. 1 minute _____
343. 3 minutes _____
344. 15 minutes _____
345. 4 hours _____
346. 7 hours _____
347. 9 a.m.   _____
348. 3 p.m.   _____
349. 8 p.m. _____
350. 5:55 p.m. [by the 24-hour clock] _____

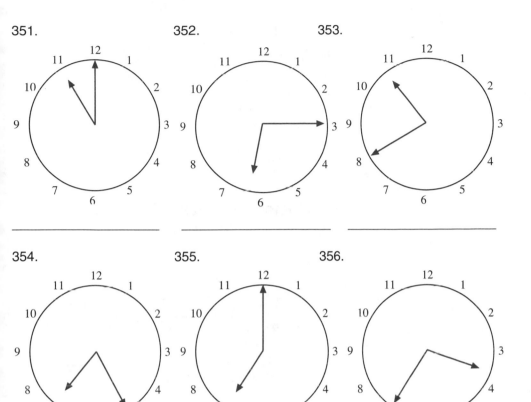

351. 352. 353.

354. 355. 356.

Translate the following sentences into Russian.

357. What time is it? _____

358. At what time? _____

§21. DATES, DAYS, MONTHS, SEASONS

Translate the following sentences into Russian.

359. Today is Friday. _____

360. Anna will call on Saturday. _____

361. Sasha will leave in the fall. _____

362. He will arrive in February. _____

363. What is today's date? _____

364. Today is October 7th. _____

365. She was born April 29th. _____
366. Today is Tuesday, December 2nd. _____
367. They went to the movies last week. _____
368. We will go to the museum this week. _____
369. I have an exam next week. _____
370. Maksim will fly to London Thursday, June 17th. _____
    _____
371. 1996 _____
372. September 5, 1992 _____
373. We were there in 1985. _____

§22. TALKING ABOUT THE WEATHER, HEALTH

Translate the following sentences into Russian.

374. It's raining. _____
375. The weather is good. _____
376. It's getting cold. _____
377. I don't feel well. _____
378. I have a headache. _____
379. I feel better. _____

Answers

§1. THE RUSSIAN ALPHABET
1. 33
2. C
3. B
4. A
5. B
6. A
7. C
8. A
9. B

§2. THE SPELLING RULES
10. False
11. False
12. True
13. False
14. True
15. True
16. False
17. False
18. True
19. True
20. False
21. False

§3. PRONUNCIATION
22. A
23. True
24. True
25. B
26. D
27. True
28. A
29. C
30. True
31. True
32. True
33. False

§4. MECHANICS
(34-36, see §4.1)
34. A
35. B
36. A

(37-38, see §4.2)
37. C
38. B

(39, see §4.3)
39. True

§5. THE ABSENCE OF ARTICLES
40. True

§6. THE ABSENCE OF THE VERB "TO BE" IN THE PRESENT TENSE
41. True
42. True
43. B
44. Это шко́ла.
45. Макси́м хоро́ший врач (до́ктор).
46. Это Ната́ша.

§7. WORD ORDER
47. A
48. False

§8. NAMES AND THE USE OF ТЫ AND ВЫ
49. False
50. True
51. B
52. A
53.

Nominative	masculine singular	Смирно́в
Prepositional	masculine singular	Смирно́ве
Prepositional	feminine singular	Смирно́вой
Prepositional	plural	Смирно́вых

54. Ивано́вым
55. Жуко́вского
56. Влади́мирович
57. Петро́вна
58. Андре́евна
59. В
60. С

§9. NOUNS
(61-72, see §9.3-1)

	Gender	Nominative Singular	Nominative Plural
61. museum	masc.	музе́й	музе́и
62. metro	neuter	метро́	метро́
63. week	fem.	неде́ля	неде́ли
64. window	neuter	окно́	о́кна
65. newspaper	fem.	газе́та	газе́ты
66. grandfather	masc.	де́душка	де́душки
67. day	masc.	день	дни
68. night	fem.	ночь	но́чи
69. chair	masc.	стул	сту́лья
70. shore	masc.	бе́рег	берега́
71. money	always plural		де́ньги
72. child	masc.	ребёнок	де́ти

(73-84, see §9.3-2)
73. Ива́на
74. телеви́зор
75. биле́ты
76. молоко́
77. ми́лю

78. на по́чту
79. в магази́н
80. на пляж
81. че́рез ме́сяц
82. за дверь
83. жа́ловался на тебя́
84. игра́ют в футбо́л

(85-102, see §9.3-3)
85. вина́
86. люде́й
87. фи́льма
88. вре́мени
89. соба́к
90. де́нег
91. мое́й сестры́
92. су́пу
93. книг
94. профе́ссора
95. о́коло неде́ли
96. по́сле войны́

	Gender	Genitive Singular	Genitive Plural
97. ла́мпа	fem.	ла́мпы	ламп
98. де́рево	neuter	де́рева	дере́вьев
99. врач	masc.	врача́	враче́й
100. иде́я	fem.	иде́и	иде́й
101. брат	masc.	бра́та	бра́тьев
102. зда́ние	neuter	зда́ния	зда́ний

(103-114, see §9.3-4)
103. в лесу́
104. в библиоте́ке
105. о вы́борах
106. игра́ет на роя́ле
107. на ста́нции

108. при дётях
109. о Макси́ме
110. на по́чте

	Gender	Prepositional Singular	Prepositional Plural
111. и́мя	neuter	и́мени	имена́х
112. це́рковь	fem.	це́ркви	цсркв́ах
113. дочь	fem.	до́чери	дочеря́х
114. сын	masc.	сы́не	сыновья́х

(115-126, see §9.3-5)
115. А́нне
116. к лаборато́рии
117. учителя́м
118. Бори́су
119. Ба́бушке
120. врача́м *or* доктора́м
121. Профе́ссору на́до *or* Профе́ссору ну́жно
122. де́тям нельзя́ бы́ло

	Gender	Dative Singular	Dative Plural
123. друг	masc.	дру́гу	друзья́м
124. сосе́д	masc.	сосе́ду	сосе́дям
125. котёнок	masc.	котёнку	котя́там
126. муж	masc.	му́жу	мужья́м

(127-138, see §9.3-6)
127. учи́телем
128. с молоко́м
129. карандашо́м
130. инжене́ром
131. авто́бусом

132. Мéжду óкнами
133. тúхим гóлосом [see §10 for adjectival endings]
134. лóжкой

	Gender	Instrumental Singular	Instrumental Plural
135. любóвь	fem.	любóвью	no plural
136. úмя	neuter	úменем	именáми
137. лю́ди	masc.	no singular	людьмú
138. лист	masc.	листóм	лúстьями

(139-146, see §9.3-1 to §9.3-6)
139. книг
140. в гóроде
141. по у́лице
142. молокó
143. математикой
144. Стол
145. мúмо теáтра
146. Сáше

§10. ADJECTIVES
(147-156, see §10.5-1)
147. мáленький стул
148. красúвая картúна
149. молодóй человéк
150. мáленькими сту́льями
151. красúвой картúны
152. молодóму человéку
153. велúк (-ó, -á, -ú)
154. бóлен, больнá, больны́
155. Я дóлжен / должнá читáть.
156. Емý ну́жен был совéт.

(157-161, see §10.5-2).
157. нáшему дóму
158. мойм письмóм
159. её сестрé
160. вáших книг
161. своя́ кóмната

(162-164, see §10.5-3)
162. это дерево
163. этой лампой
164. этот мальчик и та девочка

(165-167, see §10.5-4)
165. Чья машина на улице?
166. Чьи тетради лежат на столе?
167. Чей карандаш?

(168-170, see §10.5-5)
168. эта поездка интереснее
169. более новый самолёт
170. старший брат

(171-173, see §10.5-6)
171. величайший поэт
172. самый хороший университет
173. Он работает больше всех.

(174-176, see §10.5-7)
174. гостиная
175. взрослый
176. больной

§11. PRONOUNS
177. Они были с нами.
178. Он дал тебе деньги?
179. Мы говорили о нём.
180. О чём ты думаешь?
181. Я прочитал / прочитала статью, которую ты
     написал / написала.
182. Я не узнаю себя.
183. Мы сами всё сделали.
184. Кто-нибудь сдал экзамен?
185. Что-то лежит на полке.
186. Мы никого не видели.

§12. VERBS
(187-197, see §12.4)
187. B
188. A
189. A
190. B

191. читáл
192. решúли
193. бралá
194. засмеáлись
195. писáли
196. приходúл
197. рабóтать

(198-207, see §12.5-1)
198. игрáл
199. везлú
200. шёл
201. привы́к
202. моглá
203. упáло
204. éли
205. началá
206. отвечáл
207. пеклú

(208-220, see §12.5-2)
208. летáют
209. вúжу
210. ждём
211. встаёте
212. танцýет
213. пьют
214. поёшь
215. живёт
216. éдем
217. мóжете
218. растёт
219. хотúм
220. бегý

(221-230, see §12.5-3)
221. бýдет закрывáть
222. подýмают
223. бýдете ждать
224. полýчишь
225. сдéлаем
226. позвонúт
227. дадúте
228. встáну
229. прúмут
230. сáдем

(231-234, see §12.6 and §12.7)

231. Он хо́чет рабо́тать.
232. Андре́й уме́ет пла́вать.
233. Мы мо́жем помо́чь.
234. Они́ ко́нчили занима́ться в семь часо́в.

(235-242, see §12.8)

235. звони́
236. ду́май
237. дай
238. узнава́й
239. ля́гте
240. вста́ньте
241. дава́й танцева́ть
242. пусть она́ рабо́тает

(243-244, see §12.9)

243. Он бы сдал экза́мен, е́сли бы он занима́лся.
244. Е́сли я пое́ду в Пари́ж, я куплю́ духи́.

(245-246, see §12.10)

245. улыба́ется
246. мо́юсь

(247-254, see §12.11)

247. хо́дят
248. е́ду
249. вози́л
250. лета́ли
251. B
252. C
253. A
254. C

(255-262, see §12.12)

255. Он сел за стол.
256. Ка́ждый ве́чер, Ка́тя ложи́тся спать в де́сять часо́в.
257. Краси́вая ва́за стои́т на по́лке.
258. Они́ сидя́т за столо́м в углу́.
259. Твоё пальто́ виси́т в шкафу́.
260. Кто пове́сил моё пальто́ в шкаф?
261. Я всегда́ кладу́ газе́ты на по́лку.
262. Весно́й Ива́н сажа́ет цветы́.

(263-267, see §12.13)
263. past active participle
264. present passive participle
265. short form passive participle
266. present active participle
267. past passive participle

(268-269, see §12.14)
268. посмотрёв
269. сйдя

§13. ADVERBS
270. быстро
271. плóхо
272. вниз
273. внутрй
274. лéтом
275. нóчью
276. рéдко
277. мнóго
278. совсéм
279. слйшком
280. там
281. Почемý

§14. NUMBERS
(282-302, see §14.1)
282. трйдцать семь
283. пятьсóт шестьдесят одйн
284. две тысячи восемьсóт девянóсто четыре
285. дéсять тысяч
286. два миллиóна
287. восемнáдцать кóмнат
288. три дня
289. сéмьдесят пять книг
290. двáдцать одйн профéссор
291. сóрок домóв
292. четыре нóвых студéнта
293. пятнáдцать бóльшйх машйн
294. вóсемьдесят дéвять красйвых картйн
295. трйдцать шесть стáрых ламп
296. шестьдесят семь мáленьких детéй
297. два (masc. and neuter) and две (fem.)
298. одйн (masc.), однó (neuter), однá (fem.), однй (plural)

299. Он там был один.
300. Одни студенты пришли на лекцию, другие не пришли.
301. две трети
302. половина

(303-307, see §14.2)
303. семнадцатый, -ое, -ая, -ые
304. третий, -ье, -ья, -ьи
305. второй раз
306. восьмая улица
307. пятьдесят шестой этаж

(308-311, see §14.3)
308. обе газеты
309. оба журнала
310. нас было четверо
311. трое детей

§15. PREPOSITIONS
312. за молоком
313. на день
314. через неделю
315. за месяц
316. к доске
317. у врача

§16. CONJUNCTIONS
318. Когда
319. потому что
320. Пока
321. но
322. Если
323. ли

§17. INTERJECTIONS
324. ага
325. тс

§18. WORD FORMATION
326. В
327. A
328. В
329. A

§19. IDIOMS
330. A
331. C
332. B

§20. TELLING TIME
333. де́вять часо́в
334. без че́тверти три
335. без десяти́ двена́дцать
336. пять мину́т шесто́го
337. четы́ре часа́
338. полови́на восьмо́го
339. без двена́дцати де́вять
340. час
341. два́дцать мину́т четвёртого
342. одна́ мину́та
343. три мину́ты
344. пятна́дцать мину́т
345. четы́ре часа́
346. семь часо́в
347. де́вять часо́в утра́
348. три часа́ дня
349. во́семь часо́в ве́чера
350. семна́дцать часо́в пятьдеся́т пять мину́т
351. оди́ннадцать часо́в
352. че́тверть седьмо́го
353. без двадцати́ оди́ннадцать
354. два́дцать пять мину́т восьмо́го
355. семь часо́в
356. без двадцати́ пяти́ четы́ре
357. Кото́рый час? *or* Ско́лько сейча́с вре́мени?
358. В кото́ром часу́?

§21. DATES, DAYS, MONTHS, SEASONS
359. Сего́дня пя́тница.
360. А́нна позвони́т в суббо́ту.
361. Са́ша уе́дет о́сенью.
362. Он прие́дет в феврале́.
363. Како́е сего́дня число́?
364. Сего́дня седьмо́е октября́.
365. Она́ родила́сь два́дцать девя́того апре́ля.
366. Сего́дня вто́рник второ́е декабря́.
367. Они́ пошли́ в кино́ на про́шлой неде́ле.
368. Мы пойдём в музе́й на э́той неде́ле.

369. У меня экза́мен на сле́дующей неде́ле.
370. Макси́м полети́т в Ло́ндон в четве́рг семна́дцатого ию́ня.
371. ты́сяча девятьсо́т девяно́сто шесто́й год
372. пя́тое сентября́ ты́сяча девятьсо́т девяно́сто второ́го го́да
373. Мы там бы́ли в ты́сяча девятьсо́т во́семьдесят пя́том году́.

§22. TALKING ABOUT THE WEATHER, HEALTH

374. Идёт дождь.
375. Пого́да хоро́шая.
376. Стано́вится хо́лодно.
377. Я пло́хо себя́ чу́вствую.
378. У меня́ боли́т голова́.
379. Мне ста́ло лу́чше.

Index

References in this index are to the Brush-Up section, consisting of the Basics, the Parts of Speech, and Special Topics, indicated by the symbol § (section) in front of a number.

NOTES

NOTES

NOTES